# THE
# WORLD'S
# STUPIDEST
# CRIMINALS

# THE WORLD'S STUPIDEST CRIMINALS

A Comical Collection
of 400 Real-Life
Bumbling Burglars,
Dithering Delinquents,
and Other
Foolish Felons

## BY THE EDITORS OF FORTEAN TIMES

Cader Books • New York

**Andrews McMeel
Publishing**

Kansas City

THANK YOU for buying this Cader Book—we hope you enjoy it. And thanks as well to the store that sold you this, and the hardworking sales rep who sold it to them. It takes a lot of people to make a book (even a skinny one). Here are some of the many who were instrumental:

**Editorial:** Jackie Kramer, Jake Morrissey, Dorothy O'Brien, Nora Donaghy

**Design:** Charles Kreloff and Orit Mardkha-Tenzer

**Copy Editing/Proofing:** Renée Cafiero, Robert LeGault

**Production:** Polly Blair, Carol Coe

**Legal:** Renee Schwartz, Esq.

**Fortean Consultants:** Mike Dash, Paul Sieveking, John Innes, Steve Moore

And thanks to Bill Barker for permission to use the Schwa symbol. For more information write Box 6064, Reno, NV 89513 or visit:
http://www.theschwacorporation.com

If you would like to share any thoughts about this book, or are interested in other books by us, please write to:
CADER BOOKS
38 E. 29 Street
New York, New York 10016
Or visit our web site:
http://www.caderbooks.com

Library of Congress Catalog Card Number: 97-71639

September 1997
First Edition
99 00 01 02 BAM 10 9 8 7 6 5 4 3

**Attention: Schools and Businesses**
Andrews McMeel Publishing books are available at quantity discounts with bulk purchase for educational, business, or sales promotional use. For information, please write to: Special Sales Department, Andrews McMeel Publishing, 4520 Main Street, Kansas City, MO 64111.

# Contents

# Introduction

Crime. Real or fictional, it runs through our entire lives, filling up our newspapers and news broadcasts, captivating us in novels, TV series, and big-screen movies. Never any fun for the victims, of course; but viewed from a distance, it's amazing how hilarious, weird, or just downright stupid crime can be. As we hope to demonstrate in the following pages.

These are the takes that generally don't make it to the prime-time crime-time shows: The robberies committed using a banana; the man who stole 80,000 rolls of toilet paper; the hostage taker who wanted to hear Kermit the Frog's record played on the radio for 12 hours straight. The bunglers, the bafflers, and the bizarros...

Among the stories collected here are some of the classic tales that have appeared in the *Fortean Times: Journal of Strange Phenomena* over the years; the rest are drawn from two sections of our sprawling archives that we've classified vaguely (and on occasion our classifications can be very vague indeed!) as "odd crime" and "inept crime." Whether every single tale is true or not is hard to say, though what's certain is that each one has appeared before in print, mainly in newspapers, or has been carried by reputable wire services. Although we can't check every case, we can at least provide our sources for every tale; these can be found at the end of the book.

Even so, it has to be remembered that in recent years the press (especially the tabloids) has given way to a tendency to print unsubstantiated "contemporary legends" as if they were fact, with names and dates and places. Worse, in gathering the material for this book, it's become obvious that, in search of small "filler items," there are some journalists out there who will simply rewrite an old story, changing the names and places (usually to somewhere very far away, so it can't be checked), and then present it as "new" news. This seems to be the case particularly with crime stories. All we can do is present the earliest version of the story that comes to hand. One can only wonder what would happen if the press took such a cavalier attitude with, say, political stories. But then again, perhaps they do....

As always, grateful thanks must go to all those readers and supporters of *Fortean Times* who've sent us news clippings over the years, and without whom this book would not have been possible. They're far too numerous to mention, but we wish them a crime-free future. In particular, may their scissors and newspapers remain forever at hand. Keep sending the stuff! We love it!

—STEVE MOORE
EDITOR

# A Bunch of Bankers

From the Old West to the present day, bank robbery has been the most romanticized of crimes, seen to be carried out with skill and style. In real life, more often than not the bravado descends into buffoonery.

BANK RAIDER ROLF HORNE escaped with nearly $5,000 in February 1993, but was arrested two hours later trying to open an account at the same bank in Oslo, Norway. Teller Wilhelmina Elden said, "I couldn't believe my eyes when the same guy asked to deposit the money he'd stolen that morning." He told police later he was afraid of being robbed and wanted to put it somewhere safe.

IN FEBRUARY 1993, bank robbers in Cooperville, Ohio, drilled through a safe door, hit a brick wall, and kept on drilling. They found themselves outside in the street again.

TRAVION DAVIS, 19, suspected that police would recognize his distinctive clothing if he robbed a bank in Los Angeles in July 1993. So he stripped naked before the raid and made off with $15,000 in two shopping bags. Not surprisingly, the sight of a naked man running down back alleys with bags stuffed full of cash was distinctive enough to attract the attention of sheriff's deputies, who pursued him over several fences before grabbing him (by what we're not told) and taking him into custody.

1

IN MARCH 1990, a blind man held up a bank in Vallejo, California, and then asked the teller to guide him out of the building. She refused, and he was still groping around trying to find his way out when the police arrived.

A MAN KEPT his motor running and his parcel well in view as he passed the note to a Florida drive-in bank's cashier in October 1980. She frowned, squinted, and went away to get help. "I got a bum," the note read. "I can blow you sky height. This is a held up." As bank staff puzzled over the scrawled ultimatum, the man's nerve broke and he fled. Some hours later, he was at another drive-in bank. This time the note was typed, but the words remained wrong. The cashiers still couldn't make them out, and the man fled again, leaving behind his "bum"—a broken transistor radio.

ANOTHER ROBBER WITH a poorly written note was Anthony Doyle, who tried to hold up a Midland Bank in London, England. Gray-haired Doyle, 54 years old and 98 pounds, was armed with a candle, with which he made his pocket bulge like a gun, as he handed his note to the woman behind the counter. It read: "Sorry Luv. This is a hold up. Keep quit. God luv you. I ned cash. And it over."

When the woman finally deciphered his scrawled note, she told him he was at the information desk, with no cash register or money. Doyle then said: "This is a bank, isn't it? Get me the manager." When the manager arrived, Doyle told him to have the money ready in five minutes, when he would be back to collect it. Then he walked out to do some window-shopping. Unsurprisingly, when he returned, the police were waiting. Doyle held out his arms ready to be handcuffed and said, "Pleased to see you, lads." He was sentenced to 12 months in March 1993.

KLAUS SCHMIDT, 41, burst into a bank in Berlin, Germany, in August 1995, waved a pistol, and screamed, "Hand over the money!" The staff asked if he wanted a bag, to which he replied, "Damn right it's a real gun!" Guessing Schmidt was deaf, the manager set off the alarm, saying later, "It was ridiculously loud, but he didn't seem to notice."

After five minutes, punctuated by Schmidt's occasionally shouting, "I am a trained killer!" police arrived and arrested him. Schmidt then sued the bank, accusing them of exploiting his disability.

> Bank robber Paul Howells fell in love with the cashier he had forced to hand over the money in April 1991. So he phoned her at the bank in Nebraska to apologize, and she kept him talking long enough for police to trace the call.

IN ONE OF THOSE STORIES that sound so unlikely they might even be true, we're told that Alvin Toffeebee waited in line at an Alabama bank in February 1995, then pulled a gun and demanded cash. The bank teller told him he was in the wrong line, so Alvin waited in line for another 20 minutes, by which time the police had arrived to arrest him.

FIVE ARMED RAIDERS burst into a bank in Baku, the capital of Azerbaijan, in April 1992. Their demands for money were foiled when the staff calmly opened up the safes to reveal rows of empty shelves. Unfortunately, the robbers were let down by their ignorance of the republic's finances: No money had been delivered to any of the banks in Baku for the previous two months.

BANK MANAGER TOSHIYUKI MIKUNI really should have known better in April 1993. Deciding to burgle a branch of his own bank on the Japanese island of Hokkaido, he set off the alarm and was duly apprehended.

Also in Japan, an unemployed man of 55 entered a bank in Omiya, on the outskirts of Tokyo, in December 1993. He was carrying a bottle of gasoline and a lighter, and threatened to set the building on fire if tellers didn't fill his bag with cash. When three bank clerks tried to overpower him, he poured out the gasoline and flicked the lighter. All he succeeded in doing was setting fire to himself, and he ended up being badly injured as well as arrested.

JOHN NASHID of New York held up a bank in the Bronx and got away with $17,000 in April 1993. He then led police on a five-mile car chase through back streets, throwing fistfuls of dollars out of the window in an attempt to hold up pursuit. To a certain extent it may have worked, as $6,300 of his haul wasn't recovered; but it also left a trail for the 12 cop cars chasing him to follow.

Eventually Nashid ran from this car, dived through the plate-glass window of a nearby nursing home, and was finally captured near a garbage can at the rear of the building. He had entered the bank draped in a sheet with holes cut out for his eyes, and was immediately nicknamed "Casper the Ghost" by police.

SCOTTISH BANK ROBBER Derek McFadden was caught in June 1994 because he was too law-abiding. Gun in hand, he held up a bank at Giffnock, near Glasgow, and then raced off in his getaway car with $4,000. Despite being pursued by police, he halted at a red traffic light, where he was promptly arrested.

RODRIGO ALMEIDA WAS arrested by police in May 1993 outside the bank he had just robbed in São Paolo, Brazil. He was nailed as he waited patiently in line to phone for a getaway taxi.

THE ROBBER WHO HELD UP a bank in Pennsylvania in June 1994 was also caught within minutes. As he walked out after ordering a terrified cashier to fill his bag with money, the staff noticed that he was wearing a jacket with his name, John Edward Roberts, embroidered across the back.

IT WAS 3:45 P.M. on a July afternoon in 1993 when a man arrived at a bank in East Hartford, Connecticut. He was wearing a blue bandanna across his face and brandishing a pistol as he yanked at the door, only to find it was locked. The bank had actually closed at 3:00. After staring at the door for a few seconds, the man ran off into a small black car. Staff still inside the bank called the police, but no arrest was made.

Perhaps even later in arriving was the gang who spent the night cutting their way into a Lloyds Bank in Hampshire, England, in July 1992. They cut bars with a hydraulic saw, wrenched out a security grille, and punched a hole through a wall. The only problem was that the bank had closed down four years earlier, and the building was now empty.

THE VILLAIN in a Fort Worth, Texas, job made two major errors in December 1995. The first one was holding up a bank situated next door to a police station; the second one was wearing a ski mask as he stood in a line of customers. As a police official remarked: "It's not peculiar to wear a ski mask during a robbery, but it is a bit peculiar to wear a ski mask and stand in line." When a customer asked the bandit what he was up to, he was told to mind his own business. Instead, the customer went next door. The man was arrested as he walked out of the bank.

THE IRISHMAN appeared to be slightly drunk when he entered a bank in Macroom, County Cork, in October 1992. He shouted, "This is a stickup!" and claimed he was armed with a weapon hidden under a coat folded over his arm. Unfortunately for him the coat slipped, revealing his arm but no weapon, at which point he announced, "It's an invisible gun." He was laughed out of the bank.

—⊶

A RAIDER in Mainz, Germany, got clean away with a bag of trash in April 1995. A clerk filled his shopping bag from the wastepaper basket rather than the cash drawer, and the thief dashed off without checking.

🔒

IT WASN'T A GOOD DAY for the robber in Sunderland, England: On August 14, 1992, he arrived at Lloyds Bank at 10:00 A.M. wearing a ski mask and carrying a small pistol. His demand for cash was met with a blank refusal by cashiers, so he fled. Minutes later he tried again at a savings and loan, but the staff ducked under the counter, and he ran off again. At 11:30 he turned up at another savings and loan in Spennymoor, a few miles away. This time the staff handed over $300. As he ran off, three men tackled him, ignoring his gun, which turned out to be a water pistol. Apart from recovering the stolen cash, they pulled off his watch, ski mask, gloves, and shirt, which contained $300 of the robber's own money. The bungling bandit dived over a fence with a 20-foot drop on the other side, and was last seen hobbling away.

Mark Burrell was captured after robbing a bank in Stockwell, England, in September 1994. As soon as he walked in, he was spotted as the same man who had robbed the same bank of almost $2,000 a week earlier. He fled empty-handed but left behind his handwritten demand for cash. This was scribbled on the back of a housing application with his name and address on it. He was picked up shortly afterward.

FROM FLORENCE, ITALY, a tale in which the guards got it wrong: In April 1995, security men were all too eager to help a man with his foot in a cast as he hobbled into a bank on metal crutches. Ignoring the alarm from the metal detector at the bank's entrance, they guided the apparently disabled man to a cashier's register. There he dropped his crutches, pulled a gun, and grabbed $40,000 before sprinting away.

MICHAEL NORTON stole two security cameras from the lobby of a bank in Brooklyn in June 1993. The cops were sure it was Norton, one of the neighborhood characters, because the last pictures the cameras took showed him unscrewing them from the wall mountings. Detective Thomas Hickey set off to cruise the streets and eventually found Norton. "Hey," called Hickey. "Could you explain to me how come the bank has your picture?"

"I didn't rob the bank," Norton protested. "I just took the camera." Oops...

WHEN ROLF GORLACH saw the local newspaper's report of the bank raid in which he'd gotten away with $40,000, he called them to complain. Angrily denying that he'd carried out other bank raids, he let them know that the January 1993 robbery was his first. What he didn't know was that stunned reporters were taping the call, and police in Herford, Germany, recognized his voice. He was promptly picked up and put behind bars.

FINALLY, WE HAVE the mystery man who phoned and made an appointment to see bank manager John Nicholson about opening an account in August 1984. He arrived at the bank in Yorkshire, England, wearing a false Groucho Marx mustache, sat down facing the manager's desk, and pulled a pistol out of his sports bag. Then, pointing the gun at Nicholson, he simply sat there for several seconds in complete silence. At last he shrugged, put the gun away, peeled off his mustache and walked out of the bank with the words: "I'm off then." Precisely what the man intended remained a mystery....

# Trouble in Store

Compared to high-security targets like
banks, the local Main Street store might
seem much easier to hold up. But then some
criminals are even simpler than the crimes
they try to commit.

POLICE FIGURED all the robberies had to be the work of the same
criminal because of the similar m.o., but when the unnamed robber moved to the big city, he came unstuck. He'd already carried
out a number of robberies at suburban supermarkets in Delaware
County, Pennsylvania, during early 1991, but in March he tried to
steal cases of cigarettes from a store in northern Philadelphia. He
apparently hid in the store until it closed, and was starting to rob
the place when the cleaning crew arrived and surprised him. It
seems he'd intended to load the cigarettes into his getaway car,
parked behind the store; but even if he hadn't been disturbed, he
wouldn't have gotten very far. A police spokesman explained why
the villain fled on foot: "While he was hiding inside the store,
some street urchins from the neighborhood put his car up on
blocks and stole all four tires."

⚯

A GUNMAN GRABBED $180 from a Los Angeles shop in July
1980. As he fled, the bag containing the money burst, scattering
the cash; his shotgun fell apart, leaving the butt behind; and his
mask fell off. He returned 90 minutes later to pick up the pieces,
and walked straight into the arms of investigating police.

CLIVE BUNYAN burst into a store near Scarborough, England, brandishing a toy revolver and wearing a crash helmet and a mask. He got the shop clerk to hand over $250 and fled outside to his motorcycle. However, he'd forgotten that written on his helmet in inch-high letters was: "Clive Bunyan—Driver." He was sentenced in November 1980 to 200 hours of community service.

An absentminded bandit in Detroit, Michigan, fled empty-handed after ordering a saleswoman to empty all the money in the cash register into his tote bag. Two minutes later he came back, said, "Sorry, I forgot it," grabbed the bag and ran off again. "It must have been his first day on the job," said a policeman about the raid, which took place in September 1984.

DURING A SMASH-AND-GRAB raid on a Zurich, Switzerland, jeweler in October 1980, the thief had his finger cut off by broken glass as he scooped up a tray of rings. The police identified the digit from their fingerprint files and arrested the thief within two hours.

IN MARCH 1995, Steven Kemble was arrested in St. George, Utah, when he tried to flee after shoplifting a CD. After being briefly detained by a store clerk, he broke free, dashed out the door, and ran into a pillar in front of the shop, knocking himself unconscious.

UNEMPLOYED DAVID MORRIS, 21, from Beckenham in Kent, England, was passing the time before a date with his girlfriend when he wrote a note reading: "I have got a gun in my pocket and I'll shoot it off unless you hand over the money." He then went into three shops in West Croydon, London, and passed the note over the counter.

At a drugstore, an assistant refused to accept the note because she thought it was an obscene suggestion. Next door in a hardware store, a sales clerk shook his head and said he couldn't read English. Morris then went into a take-out restaurant, but the cashier couldn't read the note without his glasses. Morris asked for it back and hung around the street outside. Arrested soon afterward, he told the police, "I've been a twit.... I only pretended to have a gun." In February 1986, he was put on probation for two years.

—•

MR. WAZIR JIWI was the only clerk in a late-night shop in Houston, Texas, in January 1990, when he found himself looking at two pistols. "You don't need two," he told the bandit. "Why don't you sell me one of them?"

The gunman named his price at $100; Jiwi handed over the cash and was given the gun. As he placed it under the counter, he pushed a button that locked the shop door. He then agreed on a price for the other gun. The outlaw grabbed the second bundle of cash, put his other pistol on the counter, and tried to leave. When he found he couldn't get out, Jiwi told him to bring the money back and he would let him go. And he did let him go, presumably guessing that anyone that stupid would get arrested soon enough anyway.

Raiders who stole 200 sneakers from a sports shop in Alfreton, England, in December 1994 were unlikely to find a buyer, as they were all for left feet.

A DESPERATE TALE from Florida: When the deliriously named Natron Fubble attempted to rob a Miami delicatessen in March 1995, the owner broke his nose with a giant salami. The fleeing thief hid in the trunk of a car, which turned out to belong to a police undercover surveillance team. Trailing another criminal's truck, the cops didn't hear Fubble's despairing whimpers until five days later.

IN JUNE 1994, two bands of armed robbers tried to hold up a bakery at the same time in Rio de Janeiro, Brazil. One group told the other to throw away their weapons, but when neither gave in, they started shooting. The first gang to arrive got away with the cash box, containing roughly $50, but one of its three members was wounded. All the robbers escaped after the five-minute gunfight.

IN JULY 1995, an armed man in Groningen, northern Holland, handed a shopkeeper a note demanding money. The man behind the counter took one look and then wrote his own terse reply: "Bug off" (or the nearest Dutch equivalent). And the gunman did, too, fleeing empty-handed.

KNIFE-WIELDING JAMES BOULDER was caught in September 1993 when his pants fell down as he fled from a store in New Jersey that he'd just robbed. He then tripped over a fire hydrant and knocked himself out.

WHEN JOHN GREGORY came to trial in February 1983, the tale that came out was one of high farce rather than high drama. Gregory and an accomplice had attempted to rob a video shop in Feltham, England, but unfortunately they were so dense, they thought the shop's typewriter was the cash register and ordered the manager, at gunpoint, to "open it up." Even after they'd spotted their mistake, they still managed to grab only five dollars before their shotgun went off accidentally, which scared them so much they fled, dropping the cash in the shop's doorway as they did so. The net return for the robbery was no money and 4 years' youth custody.

ALMOST AS ABSURD were Clive Robertson and Paul Fletcher, who attempted to rob a New York store at gunpoint in December 1994. Having ordered everyone to freeze, Fletcher went to grab the cash from the cash register, only to be accidentally shot in the leg by Robertson. They then spent so long arguing about it that the cops arrived and hauled them off to jail.

🔒

WHEN GUNMAN Danny Wilson burst into a jeweler's in Berkshire, England, all seemed to be going well as he tied up the two members of the staff within. It was after that the trouble started. Knots obviously weren't Wilson's strong point, as the two men broke free and overpowered him. They then beat him up so seriously that he had to be taken to the hospital, where he needed 52 stitches. He also got 4½ years in jail when he appeared in court in March 1992.

In December 1992, a masked raider fled from a fish-and-chips joint in Yorkshire, England, when the assistant threw hot fries at him.

PETER HARRIS walked into a newsstand in Southampton, England, in March 1994, brandishing a gun. He demanded a plastic shopping bag, was given it with unsurprising promptness, and then staggered out of the shop. Appearing in court a few days later, he was given a year's probation.

━●

ONE OF OUR MOST INEPT STORE ROBBERS must be "Bob" of Jacksonville, Florida. In May 1991, he tried to hold up a supermarket, wearing a paper bag over his head, with eyeholes cut in it so he could see. First off he demanded that clerk Keetek Dore give him the register, which left Dore uncertain whether he wanted the entire cash register or just the money in it. While they were debating the point, the robber's bag shifted, leaving him unable to see. As he tried to adjust the bag, it ripped, exposing the face of a regular customer. "I yelled, 'Bob!'" Dore said. "Then he ran away." She was unable to say whether Bob had a weapon—he had a paper bag over his hand, too.

AN ARMED ROBBER attempting to hold up a garage near Sitting-bourne, England, in March 1995, fled with only 50 pence worth of candy, while leaving behind a ten-pound note of his own.

LASTLY, TWO TALES (and perhaps they are no more than tales) of shoplifting that went wrong. In September 1991, Joyce Lebrom fainted at a supermarket checkout in Berne, Switzerland. Staff thought she'd suffered from a heart attack, but when paramedics arrived, they found a stolen chicken stuffed down her bra. The cold had caused her to pass out, and after recovering in the hospital, she was charged with theft.

Then there was Winston Treadway, who took two live lob-sters from a tank in a supermarket in Boston, Massachusetts, in December 1994, and stuffed them down his pants. The lobsters fastened onto his manhood and refused to let go. Doctors re-portedly said the result was "a do-it-yourself vasectomy," and told him he might never be a father.

# They Took What?

Mirror, mirror, on the wall, what's the oddest theft of all? Here's a selection of bizarre booty that boggles the mind.

A RUSSIAN MAN ARRIVED at his country retreat near Arkhangelsk, Russia, on the White Sea, in August 1992, and found the entire house stolen, complete with outhouses and fences, leaving just a vegetable patch.

If that wasn't bad enough, members of a British Rail cricket team turned up for the first match of the 1978 season at their field near Kidderminster, England. The pavilion had disappeared. How one steals an eight-room building without anyone noticing remains a mystery.

—•

THE LOCATION SWITCHES to the town of Florida in Uruguay, in July 1987, where the Santa Lucua Chico River was spanned by a 160-foot iron bridge—"was" being the operative word, as it suddenly disappeared, presumably stolen, without a single bolt left behind.

TWO CAST-IRON flower pots, each weighing about 240 pounds, were stolen from the backyard of a house in Edinburgh, Scotland, in May 1990. The only way out was by a seven-foot-high locked gate. Footprints indicated that the thieves had lifted the pots, worth $1,300, over the top, despite the fact that they were filled with soil and plants. Owner Carol Duff said she was "flabbergasted," and couldn't understand why the thieves hadn't emptied out the pots before lifting them over the gate.

IN JULY 1995, it was an entire London street that turned up missing. Using a mechanical digger and trucks, thieves worked in broad daylight to excavate and carry off $176,000 worth of Victorian cobblestones from a road at a disused British Gas site. A spokesman said the company hadn't even known the cobblestones were there until a neighbor phoned to say they'd been stolen.

IN CENTRAL PARK, Hartlepool, England, thieves with power saws stole 21 newly installed metal lampposts in November 1994. Council workers found only the stumps, with the wires sticking out.

IN MARCH 1987, Edward Williams of Houston, Texas, was fined $10,000 and put on 10 years' probation. He had formerly been a storeroom supervisor at Houston's Jefferson Davis Hospital, and he had been convicted of stealing 79,680 rolls of toilet paper. No one knew for sure what he'd done with the purloined paper.

MANDY HAMMOND from Arnold, England, went out with two friends in January 1988. As they waited for a taxi, a man walked up to them and demanded Mandy's lipstick and eyeshadow. The group thought he was joking, but he then pulled a gun, held it to her friend Paul Upton's head and announced, "Don't laugh. I've got a gun, and I'll shoot if you haven't got any lipstick." Lipstick was promptly produced, and the man strolled off.

In the same month a gunman struck in Scarborough, England. Wearing a hood and dark glasses, he forced a pharmacist's assistant, at gunpoint, to fill a bag with pimple cream. Police were said to be "puzzled."

ANOTHER HOODED HOODLUM struck in Ashton-under-Lyne, England, in February 1994. This one was 3 feet, 6 inches tall and eight years old, and the target was a candy store. Having bought a bag of candy, he then produced a gun and a plastic shopping bag and told the woman behind the counter to fill it up. She wasn't actually sure whether he meant with money or candy, but she pressed an alarm anyway, and the youthful hood ran for it.

IN JUNE 1987, a crossing guard at Wantage, England, was startled when a car containing two men pulled up beside her. One of them snatched her crossing sign, and they sped away.

As if that weren't bad enough, in October 1995, the crossing guards of Leeds were losing their signs on a grand scale. Eleven had been stolen. Police said they suspected scrap-metal bandits but hadn't ruled out the possibility that a bizarre cult was using the signs in some sort of strange ritualistic ceremony. The mind boggles....

In New Jersey, similar hijinks: A man with a gun held up nine people in March 1994 and ordered them to hand over their garden spades. "This is one big weirdo on the loose," remarked an insightful policeman.

IN NOVEMBER 1980, the youthful E Gang of Winnipeg, Canada, decided to call it quits. Not a gang of drugged ravers, they'd spent several months stealing the letter E from various signs, leaving buildings identified as University of Winnip-g, R-d Cross Headquarters, and so on. The whole thing had begun when one of them found a discarded E from a cinema marquee, and publicity and press interviews followed. There were even imitators: The gang would take only one E from the same place, so the discovery of a sign reading "W-llington Tow-rs" revealed the hand of renegades.

Finally, with police stepping up the hunt for them, the gang of well-off teenagers decided to call a halt, and sent their lawyer to the police with a trunk full of different Es.

ROY PHILLIPS' DOWNFALL was the color yellow. Appearing in court on shoplifting charges in October 1980, he wore a yellow parka, yellow shirt, yellow pants, and a yellow tie. It was similar dress that drew him to the attention of the store detective at a supermarket in Oldham, England, where everything he was stealing had a yellow connection: Scotch eggs, jellies, mustard, cheese, three pairs of socks, and two pairs of underpants. He was given a one-month suspended sentence.

A CAR THIEF in Holloway, north of London, got away with something special in September 1981. Tucked away in the trunk of his car was a box containing 120 plastic earholes. They were plastic molds made for the Royal National Throat, Nose and Ear Hospital, to allow hearing aids to be tailor-made for patients. One can only imagine the thief trying to sell them on the open market: "'Ere, guv—wanna buy some plastic ear'oles?"

Adriano Terroni of Italy had to come clean in June 1992, when police found 17,000 stolen bars of hotel soap hidden under his bed.

IN A TWIST on the usual expression, burglars broke into an apartment in Niagara Falls, New York, in August 1979 and took nothing but the kitchen sink. No other property was stolen or damaged at Jennie Martelli's home, just the $70 sink.

GLASGOW BOOKSTORES were plagued by a mystery thief for more than two years, starting in 1985. He or she had only one obscure object of desire in mind: photographs of bald film star Yul Brynner. The thief apparently wandered into book departments all over the city, calmly cut out any photographs of Brynner, and vanished again. The thefts were discovered only when customers who'd bought the books took them back to complain about missing pictures.

PRESUMABLY FEELING ABSOLUTELY desperate for a smoke, in February 1995, a robber armed with a knife stole a half-smoked cigarette from a man's mouth in east London.

EX-REBEL ALLAN OMONDE appeared in court in Kumi District, Uganda, in October 1995, on the charge of stealing an old man's big edible rat. Omonde was given 12 strokes of the cane for stealing John Onyait's smoked rat, while Onyait lamented that he'd been deprived of his favorite dish. Omonde was also ordered to hunt down and trap five more edible rats as a fine payable to his elderly victim.

LABORER MAPHUPU MOLATUDI, 55, was asleep in a hostel north of Johannesburg, South Africa, in February 1996, when a robber tried to force open his mouth and steal his false teeth. Not surprisingly, Molatudi woke up, but the thief beat him with his fists, grabbed him by the throat, and took his teeth anyway. A suspect was arrested, but the teeth were not recovered.

IN MAY 1995, thieves spent an entire night unscrewing the aluminum handles from every one of 150 doors in two 19-story blocks of apartments in Birmingham, England.

THIEVES BROKE into a dental office in Hatch End, England, in May 1995. Having climbed on the roof and forced a window, they made a thorough search of the premises, ignored drugs and valuable equipment, and made off with toothbrushes and toothpaste.

# Felonious Food

Grub used as weapons, thefts of edibles,
crimes committed to appease strange
appetites, and robbers beaten off with volleys
of victuals. They're all here in this collection
of criminal comestibles.

CARL LANCASTER, 30, was jailed for 3½ years in December 1990. He had held up a Shell gas station in London, England, brandishing a plastic bag with a "long object in it," which was, in fact, a cucumber. Perhaps he should have stopped there, but no...

Two days later, flushed with success, Lancaster hailed a taxi and was driven to a grocery store, where he bought a bunch of bananas and a cucumber. Giving the driver a banana, he was then driven back to the gas station he had robbed before, donned some shades, and approached the cashier holding the cucumber inside a plastic bag. He obtained nearly $100, but his planned getaway in the taxi was blocked by angry customers. He escaped down an underpass, and police later found him in some bushes, where he claimed he was relieving himself.

Still on the subject of long green vegetables: we're told that Catherine Deck killed her husband, Alain, after a heated argument at their home in Lyon, France, in March 1993, by smacking him in the face with a giant cucumber.

—●

APTLY NAMED, perhaps, Mohammed Jabber, 33, was jailed for 3 years in November 1991, after he kidnapped a former Bangladeshi politician in London, England, and forced a chili pepper up his rectum in an argument over a debt. Jabber, a community worker, photographed the man as he suffered "considerable pain."

Perhaps it's a south Asian thing: In January 1996, a 55-year-old Sri Lankan woman fought off a would-be rapist by emptying a bottle of chili sauce over his naked body. The attacker fled and was reported to have "remained several hours under water in great pain" before being arrested.

🔒

IN JOHANNESBURG, South Africa, a shoplifter with a passion for cheese was caught for the sixth time in November 1994, after stealing gouda and cheddar. Cleopas Ntima told police he paid for his other groceries, but said "voices" told him to take the cheese.

🔑

ENTERPRISING THIEVES smashed their way into a pub in Devon, England, in August 1992, using a frozen rabbit as a battering ram. They left it on the bar to thaw out.

🔒

A ROBBER ARMED with a sausage raided a shop in Graz, Austria, and escaped with $1,600 in August 1992. Storekeeper Rudy Buckmeister was hit over the head with the ten-pound wurst. "It felt like a baseball bat," he said.

🔑

IN JANUARY 1992, Nigel Hayward was released from a 2-year sentence for robbery using a banana. The next day he walked into a bank with a banana under his shirt and a cashier gave him $470. The same trick worked at a savings and loan where he got $2,400. Later he was arrested for arguing in a Bristol nightclub named Joe Bananas, and charges for the other crimes followed. He was jailed for 6 more years.

A month later Ian Gaffney was jailed for robbing a bank in Leominster with a banana. The defense said that at the time of the raid Gaffney was "suffering from a brain problem."

THIEVES BURROWED through the wall of a Vancouver restaurant in January 1994. They ignored cash and valuables, instead stealing 500 helpings of homemade lasagna and cannelloni. "It was all they took," said Andy Mollica, owner of Anducci's Pasta Bar. "No one can figure it out."

WHEN THREE POLICEMEN set about removing an Aborigine sitting in the street trying to commit suicide outside the town of Tea Tree in Northern Australia, they were attacked by a group of 15 men who whacked them with three-foot-long frozen kangaroo tails. The policemen suffered cuts and bruises but were not seriously injured, even though they claimed the frozen tails were "lethal as a steel bar." The tails, an Aboriginal delicacy, are shipped out frozen from Adelaide, to save the locals from having to go out and kill the kangaroos themselves. Six men appeared in court the day after the attack, in March 1991, charged with assault. The tails were not introduced as evidence. It was believed they had been eaten.

A similar tale from Sacramento, California, in December of the same year: Kao Khae Saephan, 26, from Laos, took six frozen squirrels from his freezer and swung one at his Vietnamese wife, Muong, 28, during a domestic dispute. She fell against a table and received a gash above her eye, for which Saephan was booked for "spousal abuse." Squirrels are a Laotian delicacy.

Two men held up a gas station in Manchester, England, in July 1991. They were armed with a can of carrots, which they threatened to throw at the cashier, and escaped with over $150.

A MYSTERY PUMPKIN-HURLER caused terror in Brisbane, Australia, in spring 1989. The most seriously affected victim was

John Cerezo, 45, whose leg was smashed in two places by a seven-pounder hurled from a passing car.

ONE MORNING in August 1995, about 3:30 A.M., a 19-year-old man jumped into a milk truck as its driver was making a delivery in Wellington, New Zealand. Driving the stolen truck around a corner, he ran straight into a bread van. "There was milk, cream, cheese, yogurt, bread, and crates all over the place," said the local police, who apprehended the villain after a sedate chase along a local highway.

POLICE IN ANKARA, Turkey, were hunting a woman in September 1995 who staged lightning raids on flower shops, then fled after eating the heads off roses.

MEXICAN PRISONER Juan Lopez escaped from jail in January 1996 after using acidic salsa sauce from six years of jailhouse dinners to dissolve the bars on his cell window.

GEORGE CABASO, 27, had a hearty meal at a restaurant in Baguio City, in the Philippines, in October 1984. Then he walked into the kitchen and dropped a nine-inch snake into a bowl of soup, hoping to get a free dinner by lodging a complaint. He was caught in the act by the restaurant staff, who summoned the police. But while a policeman was taking down Cabaso's statement, Cabaso swallowed the snake and said, "Where is your evidence?" Cabaso was set free.

A BANK OFFICIAL who disappeared with more than $800,000 was traced in September 1994, but there was no sign of the cash. Armin Maihof had eaten the evidence. Police in Zurich, Switzerland, investigated for two years before tracking him down; but Maihof suffered from a rare condition that made him crave paper, so he'd munched his way through the money before they found him.

THIEVES STRUCK at a discount store in Kenilworth, England, in May 1995, and made off with 60 tubes of toothpaste, worth about $150. It was the tenth raid of the year in which only toothpaste was stolen. "I cannot see there being a black market for toothpaste," said a spokesman.

A police swat team swung into action in July 1995, when Jorge Amestoy was attacked in his food truck in Miami, Florida. A man tried to grab cans of black beans, bags of rice, and bottles of olive oil. In the struggle that followed, the robber threw a can of beans, which gashed Amestoy's head, then barricaded himself in the van. Armed with a knife as well as more cans of beans, the raider then proceeded to strip naked and held the cops at bay for some time before a hostage negotiator persuaded him to give himself up. He was charged with aggravated battery.

AN ARMED THIEF who tried to hold up a bakery in Kiel, Germany, in June 1995, was sent packing by a torrent of cream cakes. A shop clerk hurled a tray of freshly filled tortes into his face, then ran into the street crying for help. Passersby overpowered the cream-splattered masked raider.

MIAMI WAS TERRORIZED in May 1988 by "The Hungry Ninja Bandit," who made a habit of eating a snack in front of his victims. Dressed in black and toting a gun, on his first raid he ate some coleslaw and had a cup of tea; a few days later he ate half a banana. Apparently doing the crimes more for kicks than money, he committed his third offense against Lourdes Orango: He surprised her in her backyard and marched her indoors at gunpoint. There, in front of her two children, he used the phone to call his buddies and brag about what he was doing. Orango offered him her VCR, which he declined. Instead, he left with $60 and two orange sodas.

—●

ENGLISHMAN Allison Johnson, 47, was revealed as an alcoholic burglar with a compulsion to eat cutlery when he appeared at Lincoln Crown Court in August 1992. At the time he had eight forks and metal sections of a mop inside him. He had spent 24 years of his life in prison, and repeatedly went into restaurants on his release and ordered lavish meals. When he couldn't pay, he would tell the owners to call the police and would then eat cutlery until they arrived. He was said to be in pain and had to hold his stomach all the time, finding it hard to eat and obviously having difficulty relieving himself. Although he had been told he had only a year to live, he was sentenced to 4 years in jail.

# All Dressed Up, and...

From a mask and a cunning disguise, it's a short step to costumes. That's what the criminal caperers in this chapter were wearing as they went to work.

DRESSED AS MUPPET characters, a handful of French gangsters broke into a sanatorium at Nancy in December 1978 and relieved patients of their worldly goods to the tune of $25,000. As they fled in their stolen car, Kermit le Frog, Fozzie and pals were enthusiastically cheered on by passersby and actually waved through traffic by bemused policemen on duty.

WHEN PRINCE MONGO from the uncharted planet of Zambodia appeared in court in Memphis, Tennessee, in June 1983, the judge was not amused. The prince was wearing green body paint, golden goggles, a fur loincloth, a gas mask, and beads, and was carrying a skull under one arm. Known to the cops as Robert Hodges, he was appearing on a charge of tampering with an electricity meter; but when the judge ordered him to don more acceptable attire, the prince naturally protested. For this he got a 10-day sentence for contempt. In October of the same year, Prince Mongo ran for mayor in Memphis, although by then he'd changed his body paint to silver. Even so, he still received 2,650 votes.

ON THEIR WAY to a debate about exorcism in Bergen, Norway, two men dressed respectively as Jesus and the Devil apparently disturbed the peace of the local citizens in February 1987. The Devil was promptly arrested and fined, though "Jesus" went free. The Devil refused to pay up on the grounds that he had been discriminated against, which is where centuries of bad press gets you.

BOB BRIGGS, 24, owner of a Domino's Pizza restaurant in Independence, Missouri, dressed as a giant red rabbit and stood on the street to attract business. In August 1991, he was knocked unconscious by Bobo the Clown, who was promoting a Pizza Hut across the street. Briggs declined to press charges, which is perhaps unfortunate, as it would have made an interesting court case.

FROM BAD CLOWNS and good bunnies to quite the opposite. In April 1987, a man dressed in an all-white Easter Bunny suit and carrying a paper bag walked into a general store in Manchester, Ohio. Then he produced a gun, ordered the woman at the counter to hand over all she had in the cash register, $655, and escaped on foot.

Some years later we have Mr. Twister the Clown, alias Corey McDonald, who spent six years feeding about-to-expire parking meters in Santa Cruz, California, "to make people happy." He was finally arrested by police and fined $15, but the Santa Cruz City Council overturned the fine in October 1995. The councilors all wore red noses for the vote.

ROMANIAN POLICE arrested three teenagers in August 1992. They had been wearing white bedsheets and posing as ghosts in a cemetery at Sighetul Marmetiei, scaring passing drunks into parting with their money.

IN APRIL 1986, movie-theater owner Bert Hudson of Salem, Oregon, offered half-price tickets to see *Young Sherlock Holmes* to anyone dressed as a Hollywood film star. More than 400 people showed up in costume, but one man dressed as gangster star Edward G. Robinson pulled a gun and made off with the box-office cash.

—●

COLIN DUFF, of Weston-super-Mare, England, was walking home from a New Year's Eve party in January 1987 when he was accosted by two "schoolgirls" in fishnet stockings, garter belts, and short dresses. While he was distracted by these attractive young ladies, two accomplices dressed as rabbits bashed him over the head with a milk bottle and stole around $15. A police spokesman said they were also hunting a gorilla who watched the assault, and remarked, "I hate to think what it would be like if we had to organize a lineup."

🔒

DRESSED AS A CAT, a man robbed a tropical-fish shop in Las Vegas, Nevada, on Halloween Night, 1990. He escaped with the money but left the fish alone.

Bartender John Collins told police in Missoula, Montana, that he'd been assaulted in the early hours one night in November 1978 by a giant fly. He said he evicted a man dressed in an insect costume from his bar, but the fly, apparently angry at being shooed away, returned and swatted Collins as he mixed a drink. This done, the fly fled. Police found his pulled-off wings in a corner, but there was no sign of the body.

FIVE BANKS IN MEXICO were robbed in early 1994 by a villain whom security guards ignored because they thought he was a little boy. The robber was a three-foot midget, dressed in a cowboy outfit and riding a toy horse, who then pulled out a real gun and ordered the staff to fill his hat with money.

A NIGHT OF COMIC-BOOK violence struck Portsmouth, England, on November 8, 1985. Batman, Robin, and Superman were arrested after a mad melee in Guildhall Square, where the superhero fists flew to such effect that police reinforcements had to be called in. Later, police arrived to quell a disturbance at a nightclub in nearby Southsea, only to find more costumed heroes swapping punches. This time Spiderman, Popeye the Sailor Man, and an Australian Desert Rat were carted off to the same police station as the others.

Worse still, two raiders, both dressed as Batman, broke into a house in Echt, Holland, in February 1990. There they tied up the terrified occupant and escaped with their victim's cash.

Those with no liking for Ronald McDonald, the burger chain's clown mascot, will be pleased to hear that while stopping over for a publicity appearance in Philadelphia in July 1993, he got a cream pie in the face from animal-rights protester Robin Walker. Walker was wearing a black-and-white cow costume at the time. Unsympathetic police charged her and a fellow protester with disorderly conduct.

LEST ANYONE THINK costume crimes are a new phenomenon, we have the following tale from July 28, 1914, under the wonderful headline: "Footpad with Horse's Head Terrifies Victim." It appears that in Fort Erie, Ontario, a racetrack employee was making his way home when a "stalwart man" with the head of a horse and a flowing mane leaped out of a thicket. Brandishing a long knife and "emitting terrifying sounds," the footpad overwhelmed his victim to the extent that the man offered no resistance to the theft of his wallet, containing $30. Hurrying home, the victim found he wasn't believed, although a couple of nights later the horseheaded highwayman was seen again, trying to rob a farmer, who whipped up his horse and managed to escape.

SANTA CLAUS WAS arrested by police in Berkeley, California, in December 1980, after he held up a bank. Portly Eugene Lunden, 50, dressed in a flowing white beard and scarlet Saint Nicholas outfit, was arrested with a sackful of dollar bills after threatening to blow up the bank.

He is by no means the only rogue Santa we know of. A disgruntled investor in Pittsburgh, Pennsylvania, who was dressed as Santa Claus, kidnapped his broker from a Christmas party in December 1983. Santa was a prominent local doctor, Grover H. Phillippi, who believed that $500,000 worth of deals made by broker Robert Haye had gone sour. Accompanied by another man dressed as a chauffeur, Phillippi offered Haye a lift home from the party, then took him to a small mobile home fitted out as a torture chamber, with a mock electric chair and a six-foot pine box resembling a coffin. Haye was eventually freed after 12 days with a broken nose and minor injuries, after being interrogated and fed junk food. Police said they were lucky to find him alive.

---

FINALLY, COSTUMES OF THE MOST primitive kind. Two men, armed with a double-barreled shotgun and a knife, forced their way into a squash center in Melbourne, Australia, in August 1980, and proceeded to rob an attendant. One of them wore a cardboard box over his head, the other an orange plastic bag. The box apparently had eyeholes cut in it, but we're not actually told if the same was the case with the orange plastic bag.

# Four-Wheel Fumbles

A collection of cockamamie car crimes
and motoring mishaps where horsepower far
outweighed horse sense.

THREE YOUTHS in Amherst, Nova Scotia, broke into a used-car lot one night in February 1980. They stripped down several cars and stuffed several hundred dollars' worth of parts into their own car. Then, apparently tired by their exertions, they fell asleep in the car, only to be woken some time later by investigating police.

A somewhat similar tale from November 1994: A car thief in Wellington, New Zealand, parked and fell asleep at the wheel, and was then picked up by the law. His name was Peter Wideawake.

＊

ERIC HARRISON, 18, was released for a 72-hour Christmas furlough in 1994 from the Maloney Youth Center in Cheshire, Connecticut, where he was being held for reckless endangerment. It looked as if he was going to be late getting back on the 26th, thus risking his parole, so he did the obvious thing: He stole a car in order to get back to his cell on time. Unfortunately, he was spotted as he walked away after abandoning the car near the prison, thus adding a larceny charge to his other crimes and screwing up his parole completely.

＊

FED UP WITH his old Ford Sierra in March 1995, Craig Lambert fired seven shotgun cartridges into the troublesome car as it stood in his driveway in Gloucester, England. He was arrested and charged with criminal damage, which presumably means that it's now a crime to damage one's own property on one's own premises.

—●

IN FEBRUARY 1995, police in Fort Lauderdale, Florida, were left shaking their heads after they picked up two teenage boys in a stolen car. Mere minutes earlier, the same lads had appeared in court accused of 25 vehicle thefts. When arrested for the 26th, they said they didn't have the bus fare to get home from court.

🔒

THREE GUNMEN stole a pickup truck in Rio de Janeiro, Brazil, in July 1991, leaving owner Demetrio de Melo very worried—for the safety of the thieves. The crooks were apparently unaware of de Melo's profession, and didn't notice that the truck had a passenger. De Melo was a lion tamer, and his lioness, Linda, was aboard the truck.

A similar tale from Hammond, Louisiana: In June 1995, Mike Cyprian ducked into a restaurant to make a phone call in the early hours of the morning. He left his car with the engine running and his nine-foot python lounging uncaged inside. When he came out of the restaurant, he saw the car in a different spot, and a man running away.

—●

IN SUTTON COLDFIELD, England, a motorist left his car and went with his mother into her house, leaving his mother-in-law in the backseat and the keys in the ignition. Enter a car thief, who apparently took the car without noticing the mother-in-law on the backseat until she screamed at him. He let her out unharmed at a traffic light a little way down the road.

A more understandable mistake was made by a car thief in Chicago in May 1993, who stole a Volkswagen Beetle without noticing two-year-old Rachel Jagla asleep on the backseat. She was dropped off unharmed at a Chicago store 12 hours later. Her diaper had been changed.

JOYRIDERS STOLE a car in Amsterdam, Netherlands, in March 1994 and later abandoned it, apparently without noticing the suitcase on the backseat; and so they lost the opportunity of making off with the large quantity of money and diamonds it contained.

In Milan, Italy, though, a thief broke into a car and did steal a suitcase in January 1994, at the same time dropping a winning $32,000 lottery ticket. The car owner, however, is reported as saying that he wouldn't cash it because it would give him a bad conscience.

A MAN STOLE a milk cart from outside a hospital in Mansfield, England, in May 1993. Police set off in low-speed pursuit and caught up with the vehicle on foot. The man was arrested.

IN RHODE ISLAND, the police were less than impressed by a would-be recruit in May 1993, even if he did turn up with his own patrol car. He'd driven straight to the police station after stealing the car from the officers using it.

Still, things are worse in South Africa. There, in the year leading up to September 1995, 141 police vehicles were stolen. At nearly three a week, that does seem a mite careless....

While lightening the load of a security van by $16,000 in May 1995, two robbers in Arlington, Texas, foolishly ignored the 23 Japanese tourists nearby. Although none of the visitors spoke English, they silently handed police 39 photos of the getaway car's license plate, and the men were arrested soon after.

OCTOBER 1994 saw the theft of a nice, unobtrusive little car in Birmingham, England: Unobtrusive, that is, apart from the eight-foot-tall hedgehog on top. Owner John Davies, who used the car to advertise a children's center, described the thief as either "a blind man or a raving idiot, because it's so distinguishable."

🔒

TWO TALES OF ERRANT cranes. In March 1991, Interpol was called in after a 45-ton mobile crane, worth more than $300,000, was stolen from a construction site in Somerset, England. Quite hard to get away with unnoticed, one would have thought, but it seems that a few days after the theft, it was driven onto a ferry in Dover and taken to Zeebrugge, Belgium, after which the thief was last seen trundling around Europe in it.

The following month, in an entirely separate incident, builder Don Hanna appeared in England's Plymouth Crown Court and received a 6-month suspended sentence. The court was told how a police car had had to swerve to safety as it was overtaken, presumably at some speed, by Hanna in a stolen 50-ton crane. Hanna had apparently decided to take the crane home with him after drinking 20 pints of beer, and caused $64,000 worth of damage as he did so.

In Foggia, Italy, policeman Antonio Demma was so keen to get ahead in his job that he issued bogus traffic tickets and then paid the fines himself. He got a 6-month suspended sentence in May 1992.

CAR THIEF Scott Timothy Root of Marshall, Minnesota, was fairly easy to track, after police found his handwritten résumé under one of the seats when they recovered the vehicle. Root went to jail in September 1993.

🔑

IT SOUNDS UNLIKELY, but in June 1994 policeman Frank Riley is said to have caught a car thief as he fled on foot by making barking noises through his bullhorn and shouting, "Stop or I'll send in the dog." The thief apparently froze on the spot, and Riley made the arrest.

IN OCTOBER 1992, thieves stole a truck in South Yorkshire, England, that contained 43,000 cans of beer worth $50,000—but every single can was past its expiration date.

A TWO-WHEEL TALE, for a change: Mark Desautelle's Harley Davidson motorcycle was stolen in May 1992, and he didn't see it again until it passed him on New Jersey's Garden State Parkway the following August. He followed the bike to the town of Nanuet, stopped the rider, and offered to buy the bike for $10,000—but first he insisted on a test drive. The thief agreed, and Desautelle promptly "test drove" the bike straight to the cops, who arrested Christopher Brown and charged him with possession of stolen property.

With delicious irony, car thieves struck in June 1994 and stole British Home Secretary Michael Howard's bulletproof car while he was attending a meeting of police chiefs. The car was taken from outside the hotel at Barnsdale Bar, North Yorkshire, England, and was later found dumped with all four wheels missing.

THERE ARE SOME, it seems, who have no love for modern man's four-wheeled friend. In August 1985 a mystery pyromaniac set fires to cars in Florence, Italy, by pouring flammable liquid over them and building small bonfires underneath.

Still in Italy, February 1992 saw a more elitist car burner strike in Bologna: Leaving 352 burned-out hulks in his wake, he left beside each car a gold-embossed card reading: "I shall clear the roads of the working classes' cheap and disgusting vehicles."

In Edinburgh in October and November 1990, 11 Citroen

2CVs were the chosen targets for firebombs and vandalism. Police were baffled.

And perhaps the most baffling of all: in Gloucestershire, England, thieves kept on breaking into Vauxhall Cavaliers in January 1994, after which they simply sawed off the steering wheels and left everything else in place.

FINALLY, WE HAVE the Brazilian car thief who specialized in stealing luxury BMWs and advertised his trade by distributing calling cards to potential clients declaring his profession to be "thief." Detectives who arrested Robson Augusto do Nascimiento Araujo in August 1994 found business cards saying he worked for a fictitious firm called Thefts and Holdups Limited, at 666 Crime Street, Delinquent Gardens. Using the false name Robson Kleber Augusto, he gave his title as "Ladrao," meaning "thief."

# In Strictest Confidence

With lots of nerve and a plausible tale, it seems, you can get away with anything. The tale doesn't have to be too plausible either, as shown by these tales of cons, scams, and the marks who fell for them.

A HIGH-TECH GANG led by an elusive Russian known as Serge milked a fortune from various corporations in New York in 1992. They began by setting up two premium-rated telephone numbers, the charge-per-minute kind used by phone-sex lines. These were named Get Rich Fast, Inc. and Work For Yourself, Inc. The gang then dispatched fake messengers to pick up packages from office reception desks; when told there was no parcel waiting, the "messenger" asked the receptionist to call the office to see what was wrong.

He then dialed one of the numbers and held a long and involved conversation, in Russian, at a cost of $225 per minute. The charge was automatically transferred by the New York Telephone Company from the business victim to the accounts of Get Rich Fast or Work For Yourself. It wasn't known how much the con men made all together, but they withdrew $240,000 in cash before the police discovered the front companies. Only one "messenger" was arrested.

🔒

BACK IN 1979, a farmer in India told a neighbor how he narrowly escaped death when debris from Skylab fell on one of his fields, and to prove it he produced a lump of charred metal. Hoping to sell it to the Americans for a huge profit, the neighbor bought it for $100. When others heard the tale, they lined up to buy other chunks of metal from the farmer, who soon amassed several hundred dollars, no mean sum in India. Unfortunately, one of his victims realized he'd bought part of an old stove, and the farmer was swiftly arrested on fraud charges.

These things don't just happen in the Third World. Houston, Texas, might seem to be a place where the populace could be expected to be reasonably well-informed about space matters, yet in December 1995 police were said to be hunting a con man who'd pulled in some $25,000 selling water he claimed had been brought back from the moon.

-●

EMERGING FROM a finance firm in Penang, Malaysia, on March 15, 1988, Madame Lim Swee Siang was approached by three men, aged between 35 and 45, who showed her a stone that they claimed had "magical" powers. And perhaps it did, for the 75-year-old became dizzy and handed them the life savings of $25,000 that she had just withdrawn. She realized that she had been cheated only after the men left, but didn't report the incident until May 22, after being persuaded by her son. By that time, police in nearby Taiping had reported that three men, two in their fifties and the third in his twenties, had cheated two other women out of a total of $25,000 in cash and jewelry using a similar ploy.

🔒

IN APRIL 1995, Virginia prisoner Robert Lee Brock decided to sue himself for $5 million—then asked the state to pay because he had no income in prison. He claimed that he had violated his own civil rights by getting himself arrested, and at the same time violated his religious beliefs by drinking and then going out and doing something that got him arrested. Brock was serving 23 years for breaking and entering and grand larceny. Judge Rebecca Smith described Brock's approach as "innovative," but dismissed his claim as "totally ludicrous."

IN CHINA, Jing Taibao ran into trouble with his patented "electronic height-raising devices" at the beginning of 1989. In his native Hebei Province, 27 factories manufactured the matchbox-size device, which was then resold in Beijing at a 400 percent markup to adolescents who believed it would make them grow two to three inches taller. This, quaintly named "the greatest discovery for short people," naturally made Jing a rich man...until the complaints started.

A TV actor applied the device to the designated acupuncture points on his body: His eyes became swollen, his face ashen and pimply; his career was ruined. When his face recovered ten months later, he found that he had actually become a half-inch shorter! Another user reported that the device caused two bloody holes on his legs, which went numb. The patent was withdrawn after it was discovered that Jing had faked the results of "clinical tests" on 158 school students by using a blank report sheet and a stolen seal from a local hospital. Even so, Jing still had a patent on another device—this one to reduce weight.

Dissolving checks were at the heart of a scam that hit the U.S. in March 1988. Checks with an unusual odor and oily feel, said to "sweat and deteriorate" before rapidly turning to confetti, were turning up, drawn on accounts in Illinois, California, and Tennessee. The scheme was simple enough: A bank account was opened with a small amount of money. Then a large deposit was made with a dissolving check, and a large sum was withdrawn before the bank caught on. Banks in Chicago and Memphis lost nearly $70,000.

IN JANUARY 1991, Indonesian police arrested a man in Jogjakarta, identified only as MR, for selling "magic pencils" at $360 each. He claimed they would automatically produce correct answers in university entrance exams. They confiscated about $4,000 from sales of the pencils, which had been on offer since March 1990. MR claimed that the pencils were equipped with copper wire and electronic signals that would confuse the computers marking the exams and correct wrong answers. Dozens of students complained when the magic didn't work for them.

NORWEGIAN CON MAN Arne Aavold was fined in October 1995 for selling splinters of garden fencing to U.S. tourists, claiming they were fragments from a Viking ship that sailed to America before Columbus.

THE MAFIA were believed to have been behind a mass robbery in Italy, in October 1983, when hoax warnings of an earthquake were given in hundreds of bogus phone calls to the Naples suburb of Pozzuoli, often the scene of tremors. Up to half a million people were said to have fled their homes, which were then looted.

OFFICIALS AND NEWSMEN in Bogotá, Colombia, were left red faced over the visit of Nigerian prince Rasulu Olatoyosi, early in 1994. The prince was received with full diplomatic honors and gave numerous press conferences and newspaper interviews. The Minister for Foreign Affairs wined and dined the prince for two days, and it was only when the royal visitor had departed that officials realized that Nigeria is a republic. The man's identity remained unknown.

WHEN PATRICIA WAKELIN of Westbury-on-Trym, England, advertised her Ford Fiesta for sale, David Brice, 28, seemed like an ideal buyer. He turned up with his granny and left the old lady with Mrs. Wakelin while he took the car for a test drive...and that was the last she saw of both him and her car.

The old lady turned out not to be his granny at all, but

someone from a nursing home in Bedminster whom he'd offered to take for a drive. Brice was eventually sentenced to two years in prison in May 1995, for the car theft and a number of other con tricks.

AN IRANIAN MAN disguised as a woman cheated 18 would-be bridegrooms out of money in 1995 before a child playfully snatched away his scarf and revealed his bald head.

Also in Iran, two con men from Teheran were arrested in May 1994 for trying to sell what they said was the body of the ancient Persian king Xerxes.

The owner of a zoo in Coviha, Portugal, dressed his three children in monkey suits and displayed them as "rare Sumatran orangutans," apparently with some success. He was arrested in September 1994.

BUDDHIST MONK Luangpu Khranthaworn of Bangkok, Thailand, is probably our oldest con man, at the age of 88. In October 1994 he was reported to have conned thousands of people into believing his hen had laid a golden egg. They flocked to his temple to worship the egg and to ask it to predict lottery numbers (how it was supposed to do this is far from clear), making handsome donations at the same time. Suspicious police eventually dipped the egg in turpentine and found it was painted.

CHILDREN'S SPECIALIST Dr. Robert McCormick of Phoenix, Arizona, rammed a rod into his head to fake a gunshot wound, hammered the rod into his stomach, bruised and battered his body, then shot a .32-caliber bullet into a piece of meat and pushed the spent bullet into his stomach wound. Then he trussed himself up with rope and black plastic sheeting and waited for a passerby to find him. The faked abduction, which took place in December 1988, was intended to cash in on insurance payments. Police spent $24,000 on the hunt for his nonexistent attackers before the scam was uncovered, and unsurprisingly, the doctor ended up seeing a psychiatrist.

—●

AND FINALLY, although it sounds too good to be true, we're told that in February 1991, three Nigerians were persuaded to part with $400,000 for a statue that they wanted to take home with them and erect in a park in Lagos. They were in New York at the time, and it was only when they asked U.S. officials for advice on how to take the statue away that it was revealed that they'd bought the Statue of Liberty.

# Bungling Burglars

It's not just careless homeowners who ask for trouble...sometimes it's the burglars as well, as in these tales of inept intruders.

EASILY DISTRACTED BURGLAR Renato Pereira dos Santos broke into a São Paulo, Brazil, social club in January 1994, intending to steal music and video equipment. Once inside, he found a defrosted chicken, cooked and ate it, followed it with a carton of ice cream, and then washed down his meal with 30 glasses of beer. By that time he was so drunk, he'd forgotten the police existed, so he stretched out on a towel on the floor for a nap. He woke to find himself under arrest.

A similar tale comes from Sacramento, California, in December 1995. There burglar Brett Woolley, 25, had lined up the homeowner's stereo and other items by the front door, ready to go, but then he decided to have a bubblebath. He fell asleep in the tub, the owner returned, and the police were called to wake Woolley.

🔒

BURGLARS WHO BROKE INTO a warehouse full of fireworks in Durban, South Africa, in October 1978, are believed to have lit matches to find their way around inside. At least one man was burned to death in the explosive blaze that followed.

🔑

TWO 78-YEAR-OLD BURGLARS were caught red-handed in a house in São Paolo, Brazil, in March 1984, when the occupants of the house returned unexpectedly. The one inside was too deaf to hear the warning of his friend outside, and the lookout man was not fit enough to escape.

—●

HELEN OATES WAS awakened by a noise at 6:15 one morning in August 1991 at her house in Milton Keynes, England, but fortunately her boyfriend was there. He went downstairs to discover a whole new meaning to the word "cat burglar." A man was stuck in the cat flap in the back door, jammed in with his head and one arm through the flap. When asked what he was doing, the burglar replied that he was looking for his cat. Police were called.

🔒

FRANK MORALES found himself wedged for more than an hour in a chimney in Oceanside, California. Morales was discovered by Lawrence and Margie Beavers when they investigated shouting and banging that had woken them up at 2 A.M. on January 4, 1993. At first the Beavers couldn't figure out where the anguished cries were coming from. "Where are you?" called Margie. "Up your chimney," came the reply. "What are you doing there?" she asked. "I'm Santa Claus," responded a sooty Morales, who was dangling just below the Christmas stockings.

Police and firefighters were called, and they had a good laugh as they took souvenir pictures before demolishing the brickwork to get the dangling crook out of his predicament. Morales, described as a 42-year-old transient, was not content with his poor imitation of the well-known red-clad traveler and seasonal housebreaker: He told police he "dove into the chimney" to escape pursuit and then decided to steal the piano. "Ho, ho ho!" chortled officers as they charged him with burglary and resisting arrest.

—●

A BURGLAR WHO broke into a baker's shop in Viblach, Austria, in August 1985, found it something of an alarming experience. As he crept across the office in the dark, he was suddenly attacked by Lola the cockatoo. During the fight, the burglar knocked over a glass tank containing Egor the viper. By flashlight he saw Egor slithering across the floor, and at that moment, the baker's pet mynah, Peppino, started his favorite imitation: a doorbell. Terrified, the burglar crashed through a window, cutting himself as he escaped. Baker Robert Koloini, roused by the noise, came downstairs to find his office in chaos, but the $3,600 in his safe still intact.

—●

ANTHONY BROWN, 42, broke into a house in Fulham, England, to steal copper pipes. He cracked open a gas main, blundered around in the dark, lit a match and blew the place up. Amazingly, he survived, and more amazingly, he went on removing pipes as flames roared around him. The house was completely wrecked. The next day he returned for more and ran straight into police investigating the blast. In March 1984 he was sentenced to 4½ years.

🔒

ANOTHER HOT-NIGHT burglary in Fulham was carried out by Tony Wallcott, 19. He took off his shirt because of the heat, then fled in panic when disturbed, leaving the shirt behind. In the pocket was his *Sun* bingo card with his name, address, phone number, and occupation, which he entered as "a layabout." Police soon nabbed him; he admitted two other crimes, and got 18 months' youth custody in November 1984.

—●

IT SOUNDS UNLIKELY, but we're told that burglars who broke into a cottage in July 1988 found nothing inside, literally. It was a front, held up by scaffolding and used by HTV for filming a drama at Ewenny, near Bridgend, Wales.

🔒

CAT BURGLAR Cosimo Ceglie, 29, was confident guests would be asleep as he eased along a parapet outside the fourth floor of the Lecco Hotel in Milan, Italy. But that night in July 1986 was sticky and hot, and one guest decided more ventilation was needed. He got up, opened the window, and sent Ceglie flying. He fell four floors, breaking both his legs.

It was just one of those nights for the burglar who tried to make off with cigarettes from a club in January 1996. He was trying to navigate a cigarette machine out of the foyer of the club in South Marston, England, when he was challenged by a member of staff and forced to flee empty-handed. The barman chased him into the parking lot and rugby-tackled him; then, as they struggled, the raider's panicking accomplice reversed the stolen car over the two men, out onto the main road, and into a ditch. The barman received only minor injuries, but the burglar suffered a broken foot, knee, and thigh.

IN MAY 1993 Brian C. Jones was arrested in Norfolk, Virginia, and charged with breaking into his next-door neighbor's house, stealing a television, camera, and VCR, and then setting the house on fire, gutting it, to destroy any evidence linking him to the theft. Unfortunately, as Jones's house shared a wall with the neighbor's, his own home suffered heavy smoke damage. This opened the house to firefighters, and the neighbor's equipment was spotted inside.

DUTCH POLICE MADE an unusual burglary arrest in Amsterdam in March 1994. When the burglar broke a window on his way in, he unknowingly roused the sleeping couple, who called the police and then hid themselves in the walk-in closet. Hearing the police arrive, the thief dived into the same hiding place. Only after about five minutes did he realize the pair were in the closet with him; they'd been holding their breath before then. He had the nerve to ask them to tell the police he was an acquaintance, but after some discussion, they refused.

IN OCTOBER 1994, a 23-year-old burglar smashed his way through the ceiling of the London Leatherwear store in Bishopsgate, England, dropped down into the shop, and then found he couldn't get back up through the hole he'd created. As there were security bars on the doors and windows, he was left with no alternative but to phone the police and ask them to come and let him out. Firefighters took an hour to cut through the security grille, and then he was taken to the police station, where he spent rather more time than that behind bars.

—•

A MAN WAS FINED $300 by a court in Southport, Australia, in June 1995, for what his attorney called "the worst attempted robbery of all time." The defendant had drunk four quarts of wine and a half pint of methylated spirits before breaking into the offices of an insurance company. He stole a calculator, thinking it was a VCR. Beyond that, he had no memory of the incident.

IN AUGUST 1995, a burglar tried to force his terrified victim to down a spiked drink to keep her quiet while he ransacked her house in Kuala Lumpur, Malaysia. When the hysterical woman refused to touch it, he took a swig to prove it wasn't poisonous. Police later found him collapsed, still holding her jewels and cash.

—•

THE NONE-TOO-WELL-NAMED John Smart of Sunderland, England, was drunk and feeling guilty about spending money on booze instead of his children, so he decided to smash his way into a Woolworth's and rob it. Unfortunately, he couldn't find anything handy to break the window with, so he decided to use a nearby manhole cover. Staggering back after hurling it, he promptly fell down the manhole he'd opened. Cut, bruised, and dripping with sewer water, he ran off to get a taxi but was later arrested. In April 1994 he was given a suspended sentence and ordered to pay restitution.

MIKE SPANGLER burgled ten summer homes in an area south of Great Falls, Montana, between May and August 1993. He stole camping equipment, stereos, video tapes, computer games, and bear and sheep hides. His downfall came when he decided to leave a message in the visitors' book of one of his victims. It read: "Mr. Burglar was here. Thanks for the contributions." Police matched the handwriting with Spangler's, who then headed for the courthouse.

SOME PEOPLE just ask for it. Would-be burglars Stuart Darby and David Jones, both from Wakefield, England, appeared in court in January 1994, after being arrested outside an electrical warehouse. They had been carrying a mallet, garbage bags— and a sack marked "swag."

In September 1992, a burglar in Bristol, England, fell out of the tree he was hiding in and landed on the police as they arrived to investigate the robbery.

ONE NIGHT in March 1996, Edilber Guimaires broke into a factory in Belo Horizonte, Brazil. He stopped briefly to sniff the glue he was stealing and, in doing so dislodged two other cans, which fell to the floor and spilled their contents. When police arrived the next day, they found Guimaires asleep and glued to the floor.

AN UNINFORMED BURGLAR who stole a 300-year-old violin in September 1993 returned it to its owner's door in Munich, Germany, with a note complaining that it was out of tune. It was actually worth $80,000.

BURGLARS who broke into the home of David and Marilyn Laidler in January 1994 ignored VCRs, computer equipment, and other valuables, and went for the money box full of one-pound coins. At least that's what they appeared to be in the dark. In fact they were chocolate coins wrapped in gold foil. The coins were found in the garden of the house in Jarrow, England, where they had been scattered in disgust as the burglars left.

CINDY HARTMAN of Conway, Arkansas, knew what to do when confronted by a gun-toting burglar in her home in July 1994. She ran into him when she went to answer the phone, but he ripped the wires from the wall and ordered her into a closet. Instead she fell to her knees and asked if she could pray for him, saying: "I want you to know that God loves you and I forgive you." At this point the burglar broke down, joined her on his knees in prayer, apologized, and asked to use a shirt to wipe off his fingerprints. Then he yelled to a woman waiting in a pickup truck loaded with the loot: "We've got to unload all of this. This is a Christian home and a Christian family. We can't do this to them." Everything was returned, and the thief left his gun behind as well.

Some thefts are more baffling than others. Burglars who got past the alarm system at the Bernhardt Art Gallery in Darlington, England, in January 1996, ignored the valuable paintings on the walls and took a bag of knitting instead.

A NEW YORK BURGLAR was arrested in September 1992 after he took a photo of himself with a Polaroid camera stolen from the house. Apparently not realizing that the print took time to develop, he thought it was a dud and threw the photo into the trash. Police found it later and recognized him.

FEBRUARY 1994 found four bungling burglars ransacking a house near Rio de Janeiro, Brazil, which seems to have belonged to a drug gang. High on drugs themselves, they were searching for a nonexistent stash of gold, cash, and weapons, but then they looked outside and saw two police officers, whose presence was quite coincidental. Mistaking the cops for gang members who were about to catch them red-handed, and thinking they'd be lynched, the burglars phoned the police and asked to be rescued and arrested. The cops were only too glad to oblige.

🔒

THE AWARD for most incompetent burglar, however, must go to Carlos Carrasco, 24, of San Antonio, Texas, who was sentenced to 10 years' probation in 1992. He was having a few drinks with his friends when they ran out of booze, so Carrasco went out for more, but unfortunately it was after closing time. In attempting to pilfer a liquor store he cut his hand badly when he broke through the store's roof; then he tried to throw a bottle of whiskey out through the hole he had created, but missed, causing the bottle to fall back to the floor, shatter and set off a burglar alarm. He attempted to escape through the hole but fell back on the broken bottle, cutting himself again; got back onto the roof in the course of his getaway, and then fell off, at which point his wallet, containing his name and address, fell out of his pocket. He also left a trail of blood for the police to follow from the store to his home, which was just down the street.

# Safety First?

There are times when it seems it would be better to leave valuables lying around, because as soon as the safe door clicks shut, it becomes a temptation to thieves. A temptation, that is, for the robbers to make fools of themselves.

THE AUGUST 1980 night raid on the safe of an office in Chichester, England, began well enough. The gang stole a $4,800 speedboat, used water skis to paddle it silently across a lake, picked up their gear and paddled back to the office. But they had mistaken welding gear for cutting equipment and sealed the safe shut. The staff had to use a hammer and cold chisel for an hour to get it open again.

ROBBERS TRYING to blow open a safe in Munkebo, Denmark, in June 1987, used so much explosive that they demolished the building. The safe stayed firmly closed.

THE FIRE DEPARTMENT was called to the savings and loan in Littlehampton, England, when smoke was seen in May 1993. As they struggled through the smoke-filled building, they soon discovered the source of the blaze: a red-hot safe with a smoking hole in it and a pile of professional cutting gear on the floor beside it. Police believed the would-be safecrackers had fled when they were overcome by fumes from their gear as they tried to burn their way into the safe.

Equally unfortunate was the gang who took a safe from a travel agent in Sydney, Australia, in April 1991. They used a flaming torch to open it, and managed to incinerate the $72,000 worth of cash it contained.

IT PROBABLY SEEMED like a good idea to start with: Thieves breaking into the village post office in Wiltshire, England, in April 1994, decided not to crack the safe on the spot. Instead they tied a rope round it and proceeded to drag it off down the road behind their car. Needless to say, this made so much noise as it clattered along the street that it woke local residents, who called the police, and the culprits were duly nabbed.

A similar tale comes from Dorset, England, in March 1992. There the burglars also raided the post office and made off with the safe, dragging it away with a rope attached to the back axle of their Ford Escort. Unfortunately the axle snapped, and the gang fled, leaving both the safe and their collapsed getaway car outside the post office.

EITHER HISTORY KEEPS repeating itself or journalists keep making up the same story over and over. Raiders blew a safe in Bielefeld, Germany, in February 1979, and the entire building collapsed around them. Instead of containing cash, the safe was full of dynamite. We're told that the building also collapsed on three raiders who blew a dynamite-filled safe in Dordrecht, Holland, in April 1991; and on two men in Kyrenia, Cyprus, in May 1994. A variant came from Weitendorf, Austria, in July 1984: There, the office was in a quarry, only one thief blew himself up, and the safe was full of 1,500 detonators, rather than dynamite.

IT SEEMED THE PERFECT time for a raid: Christmas Eve 1994, with a disco next door making plenty of noise to cover any racket they might make. So two burglars broke into the Spoils shop in Southend, England, and then ransacked the offices on the floor above. Their big mistake came when they decided to drag a heavy safe into a small service elevator and take it downstairs, without noticing a sign saying that it was intended for no more than two people. Grossly overloaded, the elevator got stuck between floors, leaving the burglars sitting on the safe and expecting to spend the entire Christmas holiday in what was little more than a small steel cupboard. Fortunately, their banging and yelling for help was eventually heard by revelers leaving the disco at the end of its Christmas Eve festivities. They contacted the police department, who brought along the fire department, who turned off the power and wound the elevator down to the ground floor. The robbers were finally released after six hours, at which point they declared they had never been so pleased to see police and fire-fighters in their lives. The police were pleased to see them, too, and took them away to a nice warm cell for Christmas.

A clutch of wasted efforts: Two drunken men struggled for two hours to steal a safe from Taylor Refrigeration in Buckley, England, in March 1994. They were so determined to take away the two-ton safe that they even left the premises to fetch a hydraulic jack. Unfortunately, someone living near the plant saw them trying to haul the safe along the sidewalk and called the police, and they were caught. The safe was empty anyway. While out on bail, one of the men, Mark Douglas, was caught committing a second burglary at the plant; he was drunk that time, too.

A BURGLAR IN BREDE, Holland, battered his way through a factory roof and four inches of concrete wall in December 1994, then broke into the safe. As the factory had shut down ten years earlier, the safe was empty.

TWO MEN WERE JAILED at Wakefield, England in June 1984: They had failed to force open a factory safe, so they used a crane to hoist it onto the firm's van. Out in the countryside, they unloaded the safe, lost control of it, and let it roll down a bank into a stream. It was later recovered, unopened, and with its contents intact: a mere $36.

IT'S NOT JUST THE BAD guys who screw up, of course. In Nowra, New South Wales, Australia, on a Saturday in December 1993, thieves stole a safe containing $35,000 in cash and scratch-off lottery tickets from a newsstand. It was later found by police, hidden under a nearby building. Nicole Gore, the newsstand's manager, expected the safe to be returned immediately, but the police refused, saying they wanted to keep it under surveillance. Alas, their surveillance was of such a high standard that by Monday morning they had to report it stolen again, from under the noses of watching cops.

FINALLY, AND BEWILDERINGLY, thieves raided a security company in Bedminster, near Bristol, England, in March 1994, and made off with 13 empty safes.

# Mugs and Muggers

These accounts of street crime range
from the incompetent to the insane, the
stupid to the surprising, the misguided to
the moronic.

AFTER HE HAD BEEN ROBBED of $20 in Winnipeg, Canada, in
March 1993, Roger Morse asked for his wallet back. The mugger agreed, handed over his own wallet by mistake, and fled—
leaving Roger $250 better off.

THE PAPER HEADLINED the story "Taking the Urine," and that's
exactly what happened. In October 1984, a mugger snatched a
bag that he thought contained cash from a Mrs. Levubu, in
Krugerdorp, South Africa. Instead, he got away with ten bottles
of urine. The woman worked for a doctor and was taking them
to a laboratory to be analyzed.

There are similar tales of surprise packages. In January
1996, a robber snatched a bag from Susan Kettle in Dudley,
England. He obviously thought it held her shop's takings, but
the only thing in it was a seven-dollar frozen curry.

IN FEBRUARY 1995, thieves pushed a 33-year-old man into a
canal and stole his backpack, only to find that it was full of
stones. The walker from Solihull, England, had been using
them as training weights.

A pair of masked armed robbers thought they were snatching wages when they attacked two men leaving the Hilton National Hotel in Leeds, England, in November 1993. Instead all they got away with was a chef's hat and a turkey carcass.

PERHAPS THE WORST of these cases occurred in Berkshire, England, in October 1992. There a thief stole a shopping bag, unaware that it contained four pythons and a boa constrictor.

Still, such occurrences aren't always accidental. A businessman on his way to the bank in Essex, England, in September 1992, feared a loitering man was waiting to rob him. So he quickly switched his takings with the contents of his lunchbox, and the thief ran off with sandwiches.

TROY BREWER, a pizza deliveryman, was robbed of $50 in June 1990 by two men armed with a snapping turtle in Balch Springs, Texas. He was in a phone booth when the men came up to him, thrust the turtle toward his face, and said: "Don't move or you're going to get bit."

Much the same idea cropped up again in Camden, New Jersey, in August 1994. Clarence Gland and Kim Williams were taking a late-night stroll when a car pulled up and two men got out. One of them produced a long black snake and shoved it toward Gland's face, and while the couple stood rigid, his associate made off with cash, a personal stereo, and a wristwatch. A snake expert later identified the reptile from its description as a completely harmless rat snake. In other words, it wasn't loaded.

A GUN-TOTING MUGGER made a bad mistake in March 1994 when he held up a man who was walking home through an alley in West Virginia. Finding his victim was carrying only $13, he demanded a check for $300. The man wrote out the check, and the thief was caught the next day when he tried to cash it. As the cops said afterward: "The crook wasn't very bright."

MICHAEL SMITH was arrested in Rochester, New York, in April 1991, after botching a robbery. Using a realistic toy gun, he demanded money from a couple getting out of their car. The woman then pulled her own realistic toy gun, making Smith drop his and start begging for his life. The couple's screams finally made Smith run for it, but also brought out a neighbor, who flung a baseball bat at him, knocking him down and out.

PURSE SNATCHER Daniel Pouchin ended up in the hospital in August 1993, when he tried to rob two women in a street in Nice, France. The victims were burly transvestites who beat him up and left him with broken ribs.

IN OCTOBER 1994, a robber in Osaka, Japan, was armed with a crossbow, an axe, a stun gun, a smoke grenade, and a can of Mace when he held up three bank couriers and grabbed $1,120,000. But he was so loaded down, he tripped and was caught by a passerby.

Even more ludicrous was the case of Jay Coates of Washington, D.C., who attacked a woman at a cash machine in March 1996, taking her money and credit card. As he ran away, his pants fell down. A passing motorist saw the theft and yelled, "Hey, you can't run with your pants down like that," and photographed the man as he tried to pull his pants up. Coates was identified from the photo and arrested later.

IN APRIL 1992, a mugger who attacked a housewife in Johannesburg, South Africa, was stunned when she pulled a gun on him, locked him in the trunk of her car, and drove him to the police.

AN ITALIAN WHO TURNED to snatching handbags to finance his drug addiction came unstuck in August 1995, when he robbed his own mother by mistake. The woman was walking along the street in Bari when her son, who didn't see her face until it was too late, sped past on a motorcycle and snatched her bag. Recognizing him, his mother was so angry that she reported him to the police.

🔒

BELGIAN POLICE QUICKLY solved two Brussels street robberies in April 1996, when they heard the victims' description of the culprit: He was wearing a bright-yellow jacket and had a cast on one leg. The man was caught within 15 minutes of his second robbery.

Perhaps it was revenge: Glen Telford of Ashington, England, appeared at Bedington Court before Justice of the Peace Linda Higgs in September 1994, and was duly bailed out. Minutes later, the justice went to a cash machine and withdrew $1,600, only to have her bag snatched. As her attacker fled, she saw it was Telford, who was back in court a couple of days later and this time was remanded to custody.

TELLING NEW YORK POLICE in May 1994 that he'd been robbed of $4,000 in the street, Robin Charles went on to provide them with an extremely detailed description. The resulting composite sketch looked exactly like Charles. When Charles was arrested later, he admitted that he'd stolen the cash from his own restaurant.

🔑

MUGGER LEON GUNNING got more than he bargained for in July 1995, when he attacked Jobquir Nahir in a park in Oldham, England. She bit off his fingertip and handed it over to police, who arrested Gunning when he went to the hospital for treatment. He got 3 years in jail.

IN MILAN, ITALY, THIEVES confronted Giuseppe Tomasello and a fellow worker as they left their office with a bag of money, in June 1994. Tomasello collapsed with a heart attack, but one of the thieves jumped on him and performed CPR. Only when the thieves were sure their victim would be okay did they run off with their prize—40 million lire, about $24,000.

SHERYL STILLER and an unnamed male companion seemed like a good team when they went into action in Jersey City, New Jersey, in April 1995. They walked up to a middle-aged woman in front of a shopping mall, and while Stiller engaged the woman in conversation, her accomplice yanked the purse from her shoulder. It was only as they started to make their getaway that things started to go wrong. Their 1989 Mercury, parked nearby, failed to start, and as the couple sat there repeatedly trying to turn over the engine, witnesses phoned police. Eventually the muggers took to their heels, but the aptly named Officer Robert Eager was on their trail. He spotted Stiller running and throwing a purse over a wall, and arrested her, recovering the purse at the same time. Her companion escaped, but his identity was known to the cops.

FINALLY, THREE TALES OF snatches and pursuits. In Southsea, England, a man snatched an old lady's handbag in June 1993 and tried to escape pursuit by fleeing across Langstone Harbor while the tide was out. Instead he found himself going nowhere fast as he sank waist deep in oozing mud about 100 yards from shore. He had to be pulled out by the coast guard's special mud rescue team, after which he was taken to the hospital with hypothermia and arrested by the police.

James Cunningham of Brooklyn mugged a woman in an underpass in Queens, New York, in August 1992, knocking her down and leaving her with cuts and bruises on her knees and arms. He then fled with her purse, only to hear feet pounding the pavement behind him, and a voice calmly announcing: "I can run like this all day." The voice belonged to Bruce Bezner, who had already run seven miles when he saw the purse-snatching and decided to give chase. After three blocks, Cunningham decided not to test Bezner's stamina any further, dropped the purse, and kept going. Bezner picked up the purse and jogged back to the scene of the crime. Police picked up Cunningham not long after.

We have no names for this tale from Sydenham, London, but a man was in a bank in Feburary 1992, when approximately $130 was snatched from him. The thief bolted, and the victim gave chase, pursuing him on and off a bus, and finally catching up with him in a nearby street. There the victim was so relieved to get his wallet back that, instead of calling the police, he gave the thief a five-pound note and let him go.

# N̲o̲t̲-S̲o̲-C̲le̲an̲ Ge̲ta̲wa̲ys

First there's the crime, then there's the escape afterward—or that's the way it usually goes. But even if our villains get the first part right, the second doesn't always follow.

ONE NIGHT IN April 1993, suspected drug dealer Alfred E. Acree, 20, tried to evade capture in Charles County, Virginia, by running into the woods. Sheriff's deputies had no trouble following him, though, as he was wearing L.A. Gear's new Light Gear sneakers, with battery-powered lights that flash when the heel is pressed. Acree had cocaine worth more than $800 on him.

IN SAPPORO, NORTHERN JAPAN, a 23-year-old truck driver tied his dog to a railing in August 1994, while he tried to force open the door of a car and steal the television set inside. Unfortunately, the car's owner returned too soon and the thief ran off, leaving his dog behind. When police untied the dog, it led them straight to its master's home, where the man was arrested for attempted robbery.

IT WAS TIME for desperate measures when Craig Dodsworth's unemployment check didn't arrive in October 1993, so he decided to break into a drugstore in Barnsley, England. Unable to force the cash register open, Dodsworth decided to carry it off to his apartment, 75 yards away. Unfortunately, he didn't realize that the receipt roll was unraveling behind him, and when police arrived at the drugstore, all they had to do was follow the paper trail all the way to his home. There they found Dodsworth asleep in bed, with the unopened cash register beside him.

IT SOUNDS UNBELIEVABLE, but frogman Keith Ellis was fined $80 in March 1990, for breaking into a riverside restaurant in North Shields, England. He left behind a trail of wet footprints.

And there are other frogman bandits to be found. In Berne, Switzerland, a thief in a frogman's outfit walked into a bank in September 1992, carrying a suitcase that he claimed contained a bomb. He got $32,000, ran out of the bank, jumped into a river, and swam half a mile underwater toward his getaway car. It seemed like the perfect escape, except for one thing: He'd forgotten that every time he breathed he left a trail of bubbles from his air tank as he swam along. Police followed the bubbles and nabbed him as he crawled ashore.

PUTTING THEIR FOOT in it, literally, were Mark and Wayne Green, along with Adrian Peart, who appeared in court in November 1992, charged with taking part in a post office robbery in Langston, England. The masked gunmen stole $8,000, but one of them stepped in a pile of dog doo as he made his getaway. Police arrived rapidly on the scene, along with a sniffer dog, which quickly tracked the odorous trail to a car parked a quarter of a mile away. Forensic experts reported that traces found inside the car and near the post office were from the same dog.

IN THE LITTLE TOWN of Killarney in Queensland, Australia, 21-year-old Jason Ballard made his first attempt at burglary in January 1992. He was quite successful, stuffing his stolen goods into a beanbag chair and making so little disturbance that when his victims returned home, they didn't realize at first that they'd been burgled. Then they noticed a beanbag missing, and the start of a trail of white beads. When the police arrived, they guessed the beanbag had split as Ballard made his escape through a window, and followed the trail of white foam beads for 500 yards across the town, past the police station, to Ballard's apartment. There were no curtains on the windows, and police could see beads scattered all over the floor. Even then, when police burst in, Ballard's first question was still: "How did you find me?"

When Richard Gillis robbed a bank in Haverhill, Massachusetts, in April 1992, he got off to a bad start by writing "This is a hold-up" on a deposit slip that also bore his own name and address. Then, given a booby-trapped package that exploded and coated him in red dye, he fled, trailing red dust, on his bicycle. Police found him struggling with the bike, covered in red dye and coughing.

POLICE WERE CALLED after a break-in at a supermarket in Birmingham, England, in March 1995. They were too late to catch the raiders in the act, but there was fresh snow on the ground, so they merely followed a set of footprints to a house 200 yards away, where they found four men with stolen cigarettes and booze.

On the other hand, police in Washington had no problem tracking down a store robber who didn't leave a trace in December 1993, because there was fresh snow outside. As there were no footprints to be seen in the snow, they deduced that the robbery must have been an inside job and arrested the store clerk.

🔒

THE SHORTEST TRAIL we know of was left by Lee Hawke of Melbourne, Australia, in June 1993. Among his loot was a leaky bag of popcorn that led police to Hawke's house, next door to the scene of the crime.

IN ONE OF THOSE dubious-sounding tales, a thief denied breaking into a luminous-paint factory in Los Angeles in August 1995; then the cops took him into a darkened room, and his shoes lit up like glowworms.

🔒

MICHAEL ELLIS was jailed for burglary in Winchester, England, in September 1993. Having broken into a house, he stole a microwave oven, but when the homeowner came home, she noticed her phone had been moved. Pressing the redial button, she reached the cab company that Ellis had phoned to make his getaway. They had a record of where he had been dropped, and the cabbie identified Ellis to the police when they swooped in on his home.

🔑

FINALLY, WILDLIFE EXPERTS in Wales studying the migratory habits of a salmon with a microchip tagging device attached to its head were more than a little surprised when it apparently climbed up a riverbank and headed across dry land. The eight-pound fish was resting on a kitchen table with three others when police arrived to arrest Paul Williams, who pleaded guilty to poaching in March 1994.

# Just Their Luck

"If it wasn't for bad luck, wouldn't have no luck at all..." as the old blues number has it. And that's certainly the case with these tales of people born under a bad sign.

A 17-YEAR-OLD GIRL attempted to pass a check for $184, backed up with two pieces of ID, at a supermarket in Saanich, British Columbia, in August 1992. The cashier called the manager to approve the payment. "Is this you?" he asked. "Of course it is" was the reply.

"Well," said the manager, "then you're my ex-wife, but you don't look anything like her." The purse belonging to the manager's former spouse had been stolen earlier in the day at Durrance Lake.

🔒

DAVID SHIDLER of Des Moines, Iowa, had no idea that his credit cards and birth certificate had been stolen from a storage building in July 1994. Then a customer walked into Shidler's jewelry store, bought $3,000 worth of jewelry, and handed him his own credit card. At first Shidler thought the man shared the same name as him, but then he recognized his own signature on the card, and his own Social Security number on the man's driver's license. Police arrested David Cox, who was believed to have used Shidler's birth certificate to obtain the driver's license, and charged him with forgery.

RAYMOND SNYDER tried to cash a check at the suburban Riverside National Bank in Chicago in December 1971. As the check was blank when stolen, in order to be cashed it had to be made out to, and endorsed by, someone. Police believe Snyder picked out the name "Miles F. Huml" at random from a telephone directory, filled out the check, and went to the bank. The clerk he handed the check to was Mrs. Miles F. Huml. She sounded a silent alarm and police soon arrived to take Snyder away. "I looked at the check," said Mrs. Huml, "and I looked at the man, and I knew he wasn't my husband."

Equally out of luck were the two teenagers who, in July 1993, handed a check for $250 to bank teller Jenny Ortez in Redwood City, California. The check was in the name of her father Jose, whose checkbook had been stolen from his car some weeks previously.

—○

IN SWINDON, ENGLAND, Colin Burkitt ordered a credit card in January 1992, but it was mailed by mistake to an old address. A few days later a man walked into the TV shop managed by Burkitt, tried to buy a VCR, and handed over a credit card with Burkitt's name on it. Realizing that something was wrong, Burkitt asked for further identification, at which point the customer had the nerve to ask him to prove who he was. His nerve didn't last though, as he panicked shortly afterward and fled into the street.

🔒

FREEDOM A. HUNTER, 18, somehow obtained the driver's license of Tim Holt, a bank teller who had reported it stolen. Hunter also acquired a checkbook belonging to a couple from Lincoln, Nebraska. In June 1990, he made out one of the checks to Tim Holt for $275, then went to a drive-up bank window to cash the check. The bank teller was Holt himself. While Hunter waited for the cash, Holt called the police.

—○

BACK IN 1989, David Beresford robbed a savings and loan in Plymouth, England, of $550, using a rolled-up newspaper that he pretended was a weapon. The cashier at the time was Heather McIndoe, who happened to be married to a Criminal Investigations Department officer. Beresford was caught and sent to jail for 5 years. Within a few months of his early release, he walked into a different savings and loan in April 1993, thrust his hand into his jacket pocket, and appeared to be pointing something at the cashier. Taking no chances, she handed over nearly $400. Then she informed police that the robber was David Beresford. Although she'd changed jobs in the meantime, she was Heather McIndoe, who'd recognized him from the previous time he'd robbed her.

—●

JEFFREY PEDERSON was arguing so loudly with his girlfriend at a Toronto, Ontario, hotel in September 1990 that the desk clerk called the police. When constable Andy Hickerson arrived, he demanded identification. Pederson promptly produced credit cards and a driver's license. The trouble was, the documents had been stolen a week earlier—from Constable Hickerson's hip pocket. Pederson, needless to say, was nabbed.

A similar tale comes from February 1994, when traffic cop Douglas Skinner pulled over a motorist in Fort Dodge, Iowa, for running a red light. The driver confidently produced a full set of documents, which turned out to be Skinner's own, stolen five months earlier.

Policeman Chan Abdullah had a simple idea for a disguise in January 1993: he shaved off his mustache and then proceeded to rob a bank in Kuala Lumpur, Malaysia. Unfortunately, his ex-wife was in the bank at the time, recognized him, and turned him in to the (honest) police.

FRANCES JAMES was returning home by subway in Boston, Massachusetts, in February 1985. She had been to the hospital visiting her daughter, who was recovering from a slight gunshot wound sustained during a mugging in the Dorchester area of the city. "I just happened to sit down next to these guys," said Mrs. James, "and I heard one say, 'I pumped a broad in Dorchester last night because she wouldn't turn loose her bag.' His friend asked, 'Did you waste her?' and the youth replied, 'Nah, I don't think so. There was nothin' on TV about it.'"

Mrs. James, who worked as a guard at the Charles Street jail, followed the 14-year-old mugger off the train, found a policeman, and had the youth arrested.

FINALLY, A SLIGHTLY different tale of coincidence. A young vandal in Stockton-on-Tees, England, displayed an uncanny sense of timing in February 1994. As minister Robin Boyes addressed the congregation at the Unitarian Church on the subject of "God's spirit being in even the most badly behaved child," a brick was heard to smash through the window of his old Ford Cortina, parked outside.

# It's the Law!

For the law-abiding, there may never be a policeman around when you want one. For the criminally intent, though, they seem to be everywhere you look.

A WOULD-BE BURGLAR broke down an apartment door in Hartford, Connecticut, in January 1991. He was immediately confronted by the two police officers who lived there, and arrested on the spot.

———

SIMON NASH'S LAWYER said in court in June 1992 that his client's "offenses were characterized by extreme stupidity," and it's easy to see why. Nash, 20, thumbed a lift from a police car in Wrexham, England, at 1:00 A.M. and, when asked why he had a screwdriver sticking out of his pocket, told the inquiring officer that he'd been going to steal a car, but there'd been too many people around. He also had a pair of rubber gloves and a length of scaffolding pipe on his person and was, of course, nabbed on the spot. He appeared in court with a large bruise on his head, gained three weeks previously when he had dived into a boating pool containing only two feet of water.

———

IN OCTOBER 1980 a man was being chased by police in Southend, England. He took a wrong turn into the central police station parking lot and was trapped when the gates were shut.

COLIN BRAGGS, 21, was arrested in February 1987 when he tried to break into a car in Somerset, England. It was actually a police car, with misted-up windows, and he hadn't noticed the two policemen sitting inside.

Less stupid but more unlucky was George Pace Jr., of Lake Worth, Florida, when he tried to steal an unmarked van in January 1991. Concealed in the back of the van was Officer Ulrich Navjoks, on stakeout duty in the town's business area where several burglaries had taken place. At 3:00 A.M., he heard someone yanking at the doors trying to get into the van and at first thought it was another officer trying to play a trick on him. When he realized that no one would do that and blow his cover, he radioed for help, and Pace was captured after a short chase.

—●

AN UNLIKELY-SOUNDING tale from Turin, Italy, where in November 1993, bandit Antonio Zappalla burst through the back doors of a police station and yelled at the desk sergeant to hand over the money. He was, naturally, arrested forthwith. "We all make mistakes," he was reported as saying. "I wanted the post office next door."

🔒

A MAN WAS ARRESTED in Bangkok, Thailand, in November 1994 and charged with impersonating a police officer. Using a stolen uniform, he had spent two months posing as a traffic cop in order to extort money from motorists. He finally came unstuck when a senior officer passed by on an inspection tour and he saluted with the wrong hand.

—●

JOHN NAPOLITANO, 27, of Long Island, New York, flagged down a car at 12:50 A.M. in February 1994. He offered the two men inside crack cocaine in return for a lift home, apparently without noticing that Detectives Eugene Lopez and Chris Nealis were wearing blue jackets bearing the words "Suffolk County Police" in large white letters. The cops were on their way back from a drug bust, and apparently said, "We've got some good news and some bad news. The good news is, we're

going to take your crack. The bad news is, you're under arrest."
They then gave him a "lift" to the police precinct house, where
he was booked. A police spokesman said that Napolitano
begged the detectives not to include what they were wearing
in their report, as he didn't want to look stupid.

---

BURGLARS BLEW A HOLE in the wall of what they thought was
a supermarket office in Nice, France, in September 1993. Instead they found themselves facing police officers who were
eating in their station canteen.

---

TWO YOUNG MEN, lost while driving in east London in October 1995, decided to find a nice quiet parking lot and smoke a
joint. They found a secluded spot on Ainsley Street and lit up.
Shortly afterward, Police Constable Berry tapped on the window and asked them what they were doing smoking a joint in
the parking lot of Bethnal Green police station. They were let
off with a formal caution.

---

WINDOW CLEANERS Mark Bloomfield and John Buttimer of
Tottenham, London, saw an opportunity in July 1998. They
flagged down an unmarked van after seeing it go through a No
Entry sign, and Bloomfield told the driver: "I am a policeman
and you are an idiot. We have just observed you driving
through a No Entry sign, which is against the law. If you give
us £10, we will release you." He then pulled out what appeared to be a police-style walkie-talkie and spoke into it, saying "Control, control, this is Sierra Oscar, Sierra Oscar."

Apparently unimpressed by this, the driver asked to see
their warrant cards. "You know the ones, they look like this,"
said Detective Constable Mark Thompson, who was driving
the van packed with other detectives. Bloomfield put his head
in his hands and said, "Oh no, just my bloody luck," before being carted off to the police station.

PICKPOCKET MARIO PALUMBO thought he was going to have another good day at the races as he mingled with a 75,000-strong crowd in Monza, Italy, in 1995. Unfortunately, his chosen victim turned out to be Pietro Fontana, who was not only a cop but the head of Milan's antipickpocket squad. Apparently known as the King of the Pickpockets, Palumbo was said to have remarked on his arrest: "When they hear of this in Naples, I will die of shame."

Welfare cheat John Bilsborough of Lancashire, England, spent three years claiming unemployment benefits while working as a contract cleaner. His downfall came in 1995, when he was spotted by inspectors cleaning their own offices at the Department of Employment.

DRUNKEN DRIVER Michael Anthony Dorsey ran through at least 15 red lights and sideswiped several cars while being chased by police in Fremont, California, in July 1993. His Corvette finally came to a halt around midnight when he slammed it into a wall—the wall of the local jail.

WHEN KEVIN EDMONDS stole a bag in a wine bar opposite Scotland Yard, he thought he'd gotten away with it. Unfortunately, not only had he left behind a glass he'd been drinking from, but his victim, the aptly named Joanna Copp, was a police fingerprint expert. She dusted the glass, his prints were traced through computer records, and he got 2 years' probation in July 1992.

TWO MEN selling counterfeit perfumes toured the Riverside industrial park in Middlesbrough, England, in November 1993. They were offering top brands at just $15 a bottle, and when a receptionist offered to take some bottles upstairs, where there were 80 other workers, they thought their luck was in. It appears that they hadn't noticed a 6-by-4-foot sign above the entrance announcing that the building was the council Trading Standards Department. Oops...

EDWARD VELEZ and Jose Gonzalez made a slight mistake in December 1994 when they brought down their Cherokee aircraft, without lights, not at a small private landing strip but at Castle Air Force Base, near Merced, California. They narrowly avoided fighter jets taking off on a training exercise and, not surprisingly, were arrested on landing. Then the aircraft was searched, revealing two pounds of amphetamines the pair had been transporting, worth $12,800.

A 20-year-old drug dealer in Omaha, Nebraska, got one number wrong and accidentally paged undercover narcotics officer Sgt. Mark Langan in February 1996. Langan realized he'd been contacted by a dealer from the man's terminology, set up a meeting to buy crack cocaine, and busted his target.

JOHN GILMER of Goole, England, was arrested for drunken driving in February 1995, but the police left him alone for a moment. Seizing his opportunity, he stole the car and drove off. He would probably have gotten away with it, driving along dark Yorkshire lanes, but for one thing: He had no idea how to turn off the patrol car's flashing blue light. The police simply followed the light and arrested him when he gave up and parked by a riverbank.

IN AUGUST 1994, Joe Campbell was in such a hurry to rob the cash register of a 7-Eleven store in Oklahoma City, Oklahoma that he rudely pushed in front of two men who were ahead of him and waiting to be served. If he'd hung on until they'd made their purchases and left, and only then brandished his knife and stuck his hand in the cash register, things might have turned out better. The two were plainclothes policemen, who carted Campbell off to the cooler.

CLARISSE WYNN and Darvie Sutton made their way into a Chicago bar in December 1995 by claiming they were delivering food to a retirement party going on inside. This was simply a cover for a holdup, of course; but what they hadn't realized was that among the party-goers were over 100 police officers, who quickly subdued them when the alarm was raised. "That's what makes this job so interesting," said a police spokesman. "Dumb people."

# Escape Artists

Successes and failures—these are the tales
of the ones who got away, and the ones
who got snagged.

ROBERT SHEPARD became the first person to escape from the one-year-old South Central Regional Jail in South Charleston, West Virginia, on June 29, 1994, using a rope made of dental floss. The 34-year-old braided the floss into a rope as thick as a telephone cord and used it to scale an 18-foot cinder-block wall around a recreation yard. He had been buying a pack of floss a week from the prison store and borrowing more from other inmates. Standard packs contain about 55 yards of floss.

The 5-foot-9-inch, 155-pound prisoner apparently attached a weight to his floss rope, hurled it up to loop through the chain link fence on top of the wall, and hung from the cord while he cut through the fence with a piece of hacksaw blade. At the time, he was awaiting trial for robbing a post office and had a previous record of manslaughter and armed robbery.

Shepard was at large for over a month before recapture, and the prison authorities lost no time in removing dental floss from the prison store.

🔒

TWO PRISONERS TRIED to escape from an appearance at a court in Watford, England. Forgetting that they were handcuffed together, they ran on either side of a lamppost. Having hurtled into one another, the stunned pair was grabbed by the guard and bundled into the waiting prison van.

IN JANUARY 1985, Yilderay Abdullah was serving time in Birmingham, England's Winson Green Prison for impersonating a police officer, when he walked unchallenged through the gates, pretending to be another prisoner who was due to be released. The other prisoner was of a different race and build, and his clothes were several sizes too small for Abdullah, but no one seemed to notice. Thirty-six hours later, Abdullah turned up at the prison again, asking to be let back in!

Christopher Logan was also charged with impersonating a police officer in October 1985, and managed to escape from London's Bow Street Court—by impersonating a policeman.

━●

MORE BIZARRE STILL was the escape of "dangerous criminal" Zulkkifli Kenyon, who was wounded when he was arrested in Sumatra. He was left handcuffed in a locked hospital room with two guards on the door, but was later discovered to be missing. He had left his handcuffs behind.

Maliu Mafua escaped from a San Francisco jail in January 1996. He was recaptured when, attempting to dial 411 for directory assistance, he mistakenly dialed 911, the emergency number. Police responded to the call and realized something was wrong when they saw Mafua wearing a shirt bearing the legend: "Property of the San Mateo County Jail."

IN MARCH 1986, police in Indianapolis, Indiana, allowed a woman accused of passing $100,000 worth of bad checks to post bail with a check. Needless to say, she was off and running before they discovered the inevitable—it bounced.

CONVICTED MURDERER Allan Kinsella, appearing in a Canadian court charged with escaping from prison in October 1994, brought a countersuit against the medium-security jail, called Bath Institution. He accused them of aiding and abetting his escape: A builder had left behind a ladder, which he used to scale a fence.

LEIRE PEREIRA MELO and a fellow prisoner set up their escape by digging through a wall of the state prison in Goiania, Brazil, in July 1995. Unfortunately, while his cellmate escaped, Melo got wedged in the hole and had to shout for help from the guards. "He got stuck because he was a little on the chubby side," said the prison warden. "Well, pretty fat, in fact."

ALSO IN BRAZIL, two robbery suspects escaped from a police cell in São Paulo in December 1993, flagged down a taxi, and were back in jail within 15 minutes. Paulo Almeida and Andre da Silva dug a tunnel through the wall of the police station; but the taxi they waved down was driven by Rubens de Jesus Alves, one of their jailers, who operated a taxi on his free days. "You don't even give us a break on your day off," the prisoners moaned as Alves took them back where they belonged.

MICHAEL MICHELL escaped from Montana State Prison in January 1991, only three months before he was due for parole on a murder sentence. He stayed free until the beginning of August, when he decided to take in a baseball game in Seattle; after all, mingling with a 27,000-person crowd seemed safe enough.

Unfortunately, when he found himself standing in line for the souvenir stand, he didn't notice that the man at his shoulder was Jack McCormick, warden of the Montana State Prison, on vacation in Seattle. "I guess I'll see you back there," Michell said, giving himself up and preparing to go back to Montana for an extra 2 to 10 years.

AT THE END OF 1990 a certain Mr. Jorgen appeared on a Danish TV quiz show and easily outclassed his opponents. He was just about to take off with nearly $700 and a vacation for two in Marbella, Spain, when the producer took him aside: It seemed security wanted a word. Jorgen had been on the run for the previous 18 months, and his TV-addict prison officer had recognized him.

Relatives bribed a prison guard to smuggle a bunch of bananas to an inmate at Pecs, Hungary, in February 1993. Unfortunately, the guard ran into the prison commander, and, apparently unaware that there might be anything wrong with them, offered him his choice of the fruit. Needless to say, the commander chose the wrong banana, bit into the metal file contained within, and had the guard up on charges.

POLICE HAD VIRTUALLY given up their search for jail-breaking murderer Daniel Mitchem in April 1995. They'd searched his house near Albuquerque, New Mexico, without any luck, until his two-year-old daughter pointed to the walk-in fridge and said, "Daddy's in there." Mitchem was found shivering inside, wearing only gym shorts.

Equally cold was Paul Taylor of Vershire, Vermont, who failed to show up in January 1994 to start a sentence for assaulting a police officer. A couple of weeks went by and the police finally raided his apartment house, where they got conflicting reports: Some residents said Taylor was there, some said he wasn't.

Finally, the sheriff's men focused their attention on a large snowbank at the back of the building, where, although there was no sign of a hole or tunnel, there was a fair amount of loose snow. They started to dig, a tunnel opened up, and there was Taylor. He denied that he was hiding from the officers, though whatever other reasons he might have had for hiding in the snowbank aren't recorded.

🔒

TWO PRISONERS in Washington were caught trying to escape in February 1992 after fellow inmates complained to the guards about the noise they were making.

🔑

AN UNNAMED PRISONER attempted to escape from Stafford prison in December 1993 using the classic method: a rope made of knotted sheets. All went well to start with, as he removed a grille and security bar from a vent in a fifth-floor lavatory, then squeezed through the 10-by-11-inch gap. Then he eased himself down the sheets, only to find that he'd seriously miscalculated, and the rope was short by some 60 feet. As he couldn't get back up again, all he could do was dangle there until the fire department was summoned to his rescue.

Another rope trick that went wrong occurred at the Prison de la Santé in Paris, France, in September 1993. Max Jardon and Bruno Viar wove a rope from the soles of 50 pairs of espadrille shoes bought by mail order. They sawed through the bars of their cell and threw the rope up to the top of the outer wall, where it missed and fell into the street below.

🔑

RAYMOND HALL was recaptured within six hours after escaping from a New York prison in July 1995, having left behind some rather obvious clues. Not only had he written down his escape plan in great detail, but he'd left it behind in his cell. The police simply read: "8 P.M.: Grandpa's house, Newburgh," and waited until the punctual Hall turned up, on schedule and according to plan, and bundled him back to jail.

🔒

DOUBLE MURDERER David Graham was only too obliging when prison officers in Florida asked him to try to escape in October 1994 so they could test a new tracking dog. They even gave him a 30-minute start. Graham did his part perfectly, but the dog didn't. Local police were called in to join the search, but Graham was long gone.

A much better sniffer dog was employed at a jail in Mexico City, Mexico, in March 1993. It found Darren Brown hiding in a laundry van—which probably saved Brown a great deal of disappointment, as the laundry van's immediate destination was another prison.

Another tale from Mexico, though this one sounds more unlikely. In February 1995, prison guards in Calaya were lambasted after six inmates escaped during exercise sessions in the recreation yard. The convicts apparently bounced over the wall using a trampoline.

THREE IMPRISONED ROBBERS broke out of a new jail in Aix-en-Provence, France, in July 1993, by climbing ladders left behind by workmen. The workers had been erecting wires intended to deter helicopter-aided escapes from the prison yard, but in preventing the high-tech breakouts, they seem to have forgotten all about the low-tech ones.

—●

IN DECEMBER 1994, an unnamed man reportedly climbed the wall of Chelmsford jail, in Essex, England, from the outside. He was carrying a rope with which he intended to haul his brother out. The fellow lost his balance, fell into the jail, and was arrested as he staggered around the prison yard, dazed but unhurt.

🔒

CAR THIEF David Johnston fled from Kirkham open jail in Lancashire, England, in September 1994. He then tried to hitch a ride on the highway and was given a 15-mile ride to a service station by a police Ranger Rover. Having gotten away with that one, he bragged of his luck to the next driver who picked him up, Steve Wynder. "I hope that you don't mind," continued Johnston, "but I'm an escaped prisoner." "Not if you don't mind," Wynder replied, "that I'm a prison officer."

JEAN PAUL BARRETT was serving 33 years for forgery and fraud in Tucson, Arizona—until his somewhat premature release in December 1991. Someone faxed a faked release order to the prison authorities, and even though the document lacked coding or a phone number, no one seems to have bothered to check back before they let Barrett go. It was believed that someone had gotten hold of a real court document, whited out some of the information, copied it, then typed the false release order before faxing it. Barrett's absence wasn't discovered until three days later, when he was due for a court hearing.

IT SEEMED THE PERFECT way to keep Donald Bissel, Terry Sledge, and Brian Castleberry quiet in their cell at the Faulkner County Jail, Arkansas—let them play Monopoly. All three were awaiting trial on various theft and assault charges in November 1994, but they never got to court. Instead they used the tiny wheelbarrow playing piece from the Monopoly set as a screwdriver to remove supposedly tamper-resistant screws on an air-duct cover, then crawled through the ducts to the roof and lowered themselves three stories to the ground using a rope made of bedding. They stole a pickup truck and vanished into the distance.

# Not the Straight Dope

Growing the stuff, smuggling it, using it
to commit another type of crime—the
variations seem almost as numerous as
the types of drug employed.

MARYANN KLESCHINSKI went to court in Nashua, New Hampshire, on one drug charge and came out on two. She was in court just after Christmas 1995, on shoplifting and drug charges, when a bailiff saw a man pass something to her at the defendant's table. Thinking it might be a razor, the bailiff pried her hand open and found a paper packet of heroin. Kleschinski was charged with receiving, and James Mascetta with dispensing, a narcotic drug.

ROBERT VENTHAM took his golf clubs with him on a cannabis-buying trip to Gibraltar in August 1994, with the idea of fooling Customs as to the purpose of his visit. There being no golf courses on the Rock, Ventham appeared spectacularly conspicuous on his return, and was arrested for possession of two kilos of dope.

IN NOVEMBER 1995, a Dutch drug dealer who passed off vitamin C tablets as Ecstasy got paid in kind with 41 fake hundred-guilder notes in an Amsterdam cafe. He walked into a police station and dumped them in front of the duty officer, saying, "This stuff is worthless. You keep it."

A variant tale from Atlanta, Georgia: One evening in March 1990, Willie J. Collins walked into a police headquarters and threw a packet of crack cocaine onto the desk of Officer V. J.

Williams. He said he'd paid $20 for it and it wasn't any good; it wasn't the first time he'd paid good money for bad stuff, and he wanted his dealer arrested. Williams booked Collins for possession instead, but said, "He thought he was doing a good deed. He said he didn't want other people to get ripped off like he'd been."

—●

ANOTHER GOOD DEED went wrong in December 1995, when Scott Plumley was told by authorities in Pensacola, Florida, that they couldn't shut down neighborhood drug dealers because they lacked evidence. Plumley went down the street, bought a four-dollar bag of marijuana, and called sheriff's deputies to collect the evidence. Instead, they arrested him and left him facing a year's jail. "It is illegal to buy drugs for whatever reason," said a police spokesman.

🔒

TALES OF DRUG DEALS gone awry are legion and legendary, but a curious one comes from Salisbury, North Carolina. In June 1993, a 28-year-old man told police that he had bought cocaine from two men, and that immediately afterward they had jumped him, beaten him up, and taken $300. The assailants then phoned him later and said they'd give him his money back if he went to collect it. He said he went to get it, and they beat him up again, hitting him with a gun. Whether he got his money back and what he'd done to deserve such treatment is far from clear.

—●

ENGLISH TOURIST John McGuire planned to smuggle cannabis into Australia in early 1992 by swallowing 55 balloons filled with the stuff and walking straight past customs. Unfortunately, the plan backfired when he became so sick, he had to have the balloons removed surgically, at which point the evidence became apparent for all to see. A judge deported McGuire from Australia.

A similar ploy was apparently adopted in September 1995 by Carlos Trujillo, who swallowed 27 condoms containing $1,000 bills as he tried to smuggle his profits back to Colombia from New York. He was arrested, however, when Customs found another $75,000 hidden in a backpack and a Mickey Mouse doll, leaving one to wonder why he bothered to swallow any of it anyway.

ON CHRISTMAS EVE 1993, a customer decided to make use of a microwave oven in a Denver, Colorado, 7-Eleven. He was trying to dry out his marijuana, but somehow he'd managed to get foil-covered lottery tickets into the oven as well, which caught fire and shorted out the oven. After putting out the fire with a paper napkin, the subject fled, leaving his picture on the store video camera and the manager needing a new microwave.

🔒

NEAR BANGKOK, Thailand, Tiang Ponpa complained to police in October 1992 that he'd lost a box of valuables on a bus. He said that when he'd arrived at the bus terminal, somebody must have taken his box, and he demanded that the culprits be caught and made to pay restitution. As it happened, another passenger on the bus had mistaken Tiang's box for his own and gotten off with it at an earlier stop; realizing his mistake, he returned it unopened to the police. The trouble started when Tiang turned up to collect his box and the police did open it—and there they found nearly 13 pounds of opium sitting on top of some fruit.

In August 1995, two lions were seized from a gang of drug dealers in Rio de Janeiro, Brazil. They were being trained to attack and eat policemen.

OF COURSE, it isn't just the smugglers and dealers who get it wrong. In September 1994, customs officers intercepted the yacht *Akiba* off the coast of Newcastle-on-Tyne, England. On board were two tons of cannabis worth $8.8 million, and three crew members who were, naturally, arrested. The customs officers took the yacht in tow but then had to cut the line in heavy seas, and the yacht later sank. Forty police and customs officers sealed the beach in case the drugs washed ashore, but three days later, when it was safe, divers went down and completely failed to find the wreck, which had apparently been moved elsewhere by the tides.

Then there were the police in Amsterdam, Netherlands, who confiscated more than 16 tons of marijuana from a drug ring in February 1995, and sealed it in a haulage container that was stored in the city's Combined Terminals. The only problem was that while it was stored there, the smugglers stole it back. Not surprisingly, this embarrassing incident wasn't revealed at the time, and only came out the following December.

IN MARCH 1994, the driver of a Mercedes was sentenced to 3 years and fined 5,000 dirhams ($526) in Rabat, Morocco. Police had found 136 pounds of hashish in the car, which had a forged registration bearing the same number as a limousine owned by Prime Minister Karim Lamrani.

THIEVES WHO RAIDED a field full of commercially grown cannabis plants in September 1993 would have found their haul useless as a narcotic. The plants were being farmed at Essex, England, under special license, and were intended for paper making, not smoking.

DEREK WALDER of Kent, England, came back from vacation to find notes from the police telling him that while he was away he had been burgled; and to make matters worse, he was also going to be arrested. Police investigating the burglary had entered his apartment and found a number of cannabis plants growing there. He was fined $3,200 by magistrates in April 1995.

A TERRIFYING-IF-TRUE tale from August 1978: Two teenage campers came across a secret crop of marijuana in the mountains near San Diego, California, but were caught by the growers, who tied them to a tree that was infested with flesh-eating ants, said to strip people to the bone in a matter of hours. Yet after an hour the teenage wife of one of the growers had second thoughts and freed the boys, who, unsurprisingly, went to the authorities. Six people were arrested, including the wife.

IN THE LATTER PART OF 1992, a gang of transvestites in Thailand robbed tourists by enticing them to suck their tranquilizer-laced nipples, thus putting them to sleep, which suggests those tranquilizers must have been damned strong!

Bangkok police said they'd been told the ploy was adopted because "many customers did not drink." Four transvestites and a woman were arrested after complaints from a Syrian and a Hong Kong man, who said they were robbed of a Rolex watch and nearly $3,200 in cash.

**Early in 1994, a number of fat women were arrested in Michigan for smuggling drugs to men in prison—by hiding the dope in the folds of their flesh.**

FINALLY, A COUPLE OF TALES of the effects of the antidepressant Prozac. Jason Wayne Laberge was on the drug in 1992 when he opened a cage in a downtown zoo in Toronto to set free some flamingos. When they refused to leave, he beat six of them to death with a broom handle. He got 8 months in jail and was ordered to pay $7,200.

An even worse tale was uncovered, along with bite-sized chunks of flesh, in the San Francisco home of Mildred Mortenson, 87, in November 1991. Police said she was being "cannibalized" by her daughter Barbara, 61, who had dried blood covering her face and was wearing a nightgown completely soaked in blood at the front. The daughter claimed she had been taking Prozac, and was treated in the hospital for a cut before being booked on charges of attempted homicide, assault with a deadly weapon (her teeth), aggravated assault, mayhem, and infliction of physical pain on a senior citizen. Her mother was also taken to the hospital, where she was in stable but critical condition, with at least 20 bites on her face and arms. Several of the bites were bone deep.

# Bizarre Break-Ins

Not all break-ins result in chaos and loss
of property; in fact there are some forced
entries that seem positively beneficial.
Others, though, are just baffling.

POLICE WERE SAID to be stumped in September 1974 by a
strange theft in Chesham, England. Many pieces of expensive
equipment and other items normally preferred by thieves with
more orthodox tastes were left untouched. What was missing,
though, was the living-room door—said to be a "perfectly ordinary door," except, of course, that it wasn't there anymore.

🔒

EMPLOYEES ARRIVING for work at a factory in Newhaven, England, found the door broken, mirrors smashed, and office ransacked. They also found Christof Pescay of Paris, fast asleep on
a sofa, wearing only a pair of shorts and sporting oven mitts on
his feet. Appearing in court in July 1995, Pescay admitted burglary with intent to steal, and it was revealed that he had a history of depressive illness and no money. He was provided with
clothing from a charity shop, conditionally discharged, and told
to get the next ferry back to France.

🔑

JANUARY 1988 saw a series of burglaries in Rotherham and
Doncaster, England. Whatever was taken, there was one com-
mon factor: The burglar had a trademark of turning back the
corners of the bedsheet before he left. Police said, "There's no
other explanation than he had a fetish for bedclothes."

A MAN APPEARED in court in October 1982 accused of using a knife and fork to try to break into a restaurant in East Sheen, England. He told police, "I wanted something to eat."

A MASAI TRIBESMAN walked into the offices of the Ministry of Tourism in Nairobi, Kenya, in February 1984, broke into a glass cage containing a stuffed lion, and began "strangling" it. When arrested, he explained that his brother had been killed by a lion and he wanted revenge.

THIEVES WHO BROKE into Bill Holland's tool shed in Dale Abbey, England, in June 1992 ignored $15,000 worth of gear and took a hacksaw to the cage containing his Rottweiler guard dog, Hattie. Then they made off with the $450 "devil dog," leaving Bill to muse: "It's too daft for words. She didn't even put up a fight."

By contrast, the house of Ronald Mills in Bath, England, was broken into in September 1987. Nothing was stolen, but the kitchen floor was littered with empty dog-food cans that had been chopped open with an axe.

A HOUSE IN GILROY, California, was broken into in October 1987. The burglar hung new curtains, made the bed, dumped the trash, did the dishes, stacked newspapers, put away the ironing board and put dirty clothes in a hamper. Nothing was taken except the old curtains. A note was found, saying: "Dear Sir, I hope you don't mind. I cleaned your house. Don't worry. I won't take anything because my father is a Duke in Spain. Don't worry. I'll clean your house for as long as you live here." It was signed "Prince Eddie." A few days later, it was announced that police would not seek charges against a "mentally disturbed youth."

WHEN ELIZABETH HOWELL BOYKINS, 25, returned to her apartment in Charleston, South Carolina, after a weekend trip in July 1990, she found another woman living there, and wearing her clothes. The intruder greeted Ms. Boykins, took her luggage, and slammed the door in her face.

"I thought I was going crazy," said Ms. Boykins. "The woman took all of my paintings off the walls, and bought a new lamp and a shower curtain and a rug for the bathroom."

The police were called, but the stranger insisted it was her apartment. She gave herself away when she misidentified the owner of the apartment building and said that John Wayne was taking her to dinner. She was detained for psychiatric evaluation.

A THIEF BROKE into a house in Renfrew, Scotland, in August 1992, and left a strange calling card: a casket containing the ashes of a woman called Georgina D. Collingwood. The police (and everyone else) were baffled.

Even so, the files have a match for this, from Boynton Beach, Florida: There Nathan Radlich, 74, returned home in May 1993 and found his bathroom window missing. None of the obvious things like electronic gadgets had been stolen, but he found his fishing-tackle box thrown on the bed with the lid open. The box had contained the cremated remains of his sister Gertrude, who had died three years previously. Police guessed that the thief had mistaken the wrapped grayish-white powder for cocaine. How Nathan felt about his sister going up someone else's nose, or why he kept her ashes with his fishing tackle, is not recorded.

HAVING BROKEN INTO a Hong Kong garment factory and found nothing worth stealing, burglar Yu Kin-fong left a note saying: "Put some money here next time or I'll set fire to your factory. You make me do this for nothing. I can't even find 10¢." He was tracked down and sentenced to 3 years in December 1994.

IN WHARNCLIFF, West Virginia, 53-year-old Joe Toler was known as a snappy dresser until a burglary in September 1982. Apart from 25 silver dollars, the only items missing were all the buttons off Joe's 40 sports coats, blazers, and suits.

BURGLARS BROKE INTO a retiree's bungalow in Newcastle, England, in October 1983. They stole $1.12 and her false teeth.

🔒

FOR MEGAN LEWIS, 58, of Swansea, Wales, there was rather more to the break-in than the shock of being confronted by a knife-wielding burglar: When his mask slipped, the thief was revealed as her own son, David, 21. Young Lewis was sentenced to 15 months in May 1994.

Police in Indiana were baffled in March 1994 by a burglar with a baby fetish. He (or she) robbed five homes within two weeks but ignored money and valuables, instead making off with rattles, teething rings, and diapers.

GLORIA SMILLIE, 55, opened the door to find a reformed burglar in his twenties standing on her doorstep in June 1995. Returning to the scene of his crimes in Westcliff, England, the young man said he had found God, apologized to her and handed her a shopping bag containing a silver coffee pot, creamer, and sugar bowl. Unfortunately, he'd gone to the wrong house; Ms. Smillie hadn't been his victim.

🔒

TWO BURGLARS RAIDING the Brown family home in Coventry, England, in February 1996 got a little help from four-year-old Russell Brown. He got up to investigate when he heard a noise at 3:00 A.M., but the strangers he found in the darkened living room whispered that they were friends of his mommy and daddy who had come to borrow the stereo, VCR, and TV, but didn't want to disturb them because it was so late. Russell was delighted to help, and held the back door open for his visitors as they left with their haul, before going back upstairs to bed. The men were later arrested and the property recovered.

THE OWNERS OF a home in Loganville, Georgia, returned home in the early hours of the morning at the end of July 1993, to find their home had been broken into again. The burglar had helped himself to grape juice and lunch meat, leaving scraps of food scattered about the kitchen, and taken a shower. The homeowners told police it was the tenth time in July that someone had broken into their house, eaten food, and showered.

A similar mess on a larger scale: In March 1995, a primary school in Rochdale, England, was left to clean up after burglars had a food fight with $3,200 worth of school dinners from the kitchen's refrigerators.

—o

BURGLARS IGNORED tape recorders, typewriters, and petty cash when they broke into a lawyer's office near Southampton, England, in February 1982. Instead, they stole a new burglar alarm that was awaiting installation.

🔒

THERE THE POLICE WERE, right in the middle of "Operation Bull's-Eye," a huge antiburglary campaign, and in January 1995, someone left a window open at the London Road police station in Kettering, England. Provide an opportunity like that and someone will take advantage of it, reaching in to steal police radios, official papers, a briefcase, and a radar speed gun. Sensitive police imposed a news blackout on the robbery, but that turned out to be as effective as their security measures, and the story hit the papers a few days later.

In a similar vein, someone broke into the Brooklyn Correctional Facility in New York in May 1986. The burglar jimmied a filing cabinet in the jail's personnel office and made off with $1,920 worth of prison officers' meal money.

—o

POLICE ARRESTED two men for breaking into offices in London, in November 1991. The burglars were given a list of lawyers who'd be willing to take their case, and picked a firm called Wyman & Walters. This wasn't the wisest of choices, as Wyman & Walters occupied the offices the men had tried to burgle.

# The Mad and the Bad

"Not guilty by reason of insanity" could be the plea in most of the following cases—or maybe not. Either way, there's some very odd criminal behavior on display here.

ELDERLY GREEK COUPLE Antonio and Fevronia Lorentzos were sentenced to three months in January 1981, for assault and disrespect for a religious service. After Costas Trontzos had ditched their daughter for another woman, they attacked him as he walked down the aisle with his new bride and smothered him with yogurt. They apparently believed this would restore their daughter's dignity.

IN DECEMBER 1982 a man scaled a ten-foot wall at the Honolulu Zoo, stripped to his underwear, and played the harmonica to an elephant. Empress, the 51-year-old female Indian elephant, apparently didn't like the music and cornered the man. He was arrested and charged with cruelty to animals.

DEANNA BALDESI, 24, was standing outside her apartment in Milan in December 1984, all dressed up and waiting for a taxi to take her to a party. Suddenly a car pulled up and a man aged about 30 got out, brandished a knife, and forced her to get into the car. He drove to a park, ordered her to strip, seized her clothes, and sped off, having explained that he wanted to take his girlfriend out, but she didn't have anything nice to wear.

IN APRIL 1987, three smartly dressed Japanese in business suits simultaneously sprayed excrement in three branches of the Sumitomo Bank in Tokyo's business district. They were arrested but refused to answer any questions.

—●

IN SEARCY COUNTY, Arkansas, Sheriff Kent Griggs was called to a rural home in January 1992, to investigate complaints that the owner, Howard Rosenbaum, had threatened relatives over the phone. When he arrived, Griggs found the house burned to the ground and Rosenbaum standing with two other men. All three were stark naked, with all their body hair shaved off. Rosenbaum admitted to burning down his house, but referred further questions to a nearby chicken, which he said housed the spirit of his dead grandmother.

🔒

IN DECEMBER 1984, police in Chicago insisted that three members of a gang who carried out the random killing of a customer at a hot dog stand had staged and timed the murder so it would make the 10:00 P.M. news. It seems they had felt overlooked in all the publicity a rival gang got when they murdered a local basketball star.

—●

DAVID LYNN JUSTICE, 21, was sentenced to 30 years in June 1995. He had abducted two women at gunpoint outside a restaurant in Houston, Texas, in December 1993. Justice forced them to buy Twinkies and caffeine pills, then made them accompany him on a tour of the Christmas lights. He was said to be depressed and wanting some company.

🔒

THE DAY AFTER WINNING $640,000 in Italy's national lottery, Flavio Maestrini was arrested for stealing $400 from a shop. Appearing in court in March 1994, he explained that he didn't enjoy spending money unless it was stolen.

IN JUNE 1992, police in Melbourne, Australia, said they believed a "gray-haired man wearing nothing but a red construction worker's helmet and carrying a white teddy bear" had started a fire at a child-care center. What with wasn't mentioned.

Perhaps they're funny about stuffed animals in the Antipodes. Matthew McFarlane of Rotorua, New Zealand, pleaded guilty in November 1995 to stealing a toy sheep from a shop and taking it dancing at a nightclub. He was drunk at the time, and he discovered when he leaned against the door that the shop had been left unlocked. Two teddy bears were also stolen, but we don't know if they had as good a time as the sheep.

And still in New Zealand, we have the 21-year-old Muppet fan who took a radio-station chief hostage in March 1996 because he wanted to hear a song by Kermit the Frog. In fact, he wanted to hear the song "Rainbow Connection" played nonstop for 12 hours. Police cordoned off the station in Wanganui and evacuated several buildings when the man said he had a bomb. It was later found to be fake, and the cops stormed the station and arrested him.

JAN MULDER OF ROTTERDAM, Holland, was jailed in June 1995 for stopping young women in the street and asking for their panty hose to use as a fan belt for his car. He didn't have a car.

—●

IN OCTOBER 1994, police in Bury St. Edmunds, England, were looking for the person responsible for completely wallpapering a woman's brand-new white Ford Escort. It had been covered in paste and papered over while parked, causing scratches and damage to the bodywork.

ORVALL WYATT LOYD was sentenced to 5 years' jail time for second-degree murder in Virginia Beach, Virginia, in January 1982. He said he had hacked his mother-in-law to death because he mistook her for a large raccoon, and from the shortness of the sentence, we can only imagine that the court believed him.

🔒

IN THE TASMANIAN town of Launceton, Don Desmond Davey was fined $1,600 in October 1995 for quacking like a duck on his radio transmitter. He was convicted of broadcasting something that was not speech, and ordered to hand over his radio as well.

Shortly before, in June 1995, Barry Brownless of London was fined $1,600 for barking at a police dog. He was found guilty of using threatening behavior.

🔑

WILLIAM BOWEN WAS arrested and charged with drunken driving in June 1986 after police spotted his car weaving on the road in Louisville, Kentucky. Bowen had his excuse ready, though: As he's legally blind, he wasn't really the driver—his dog, Sir Anheuser Busch, II, was. Bowen had had an argument with his girlfriend, who had left him at a tavern with the car and the dog. As he had to get home, he sat the dog in the passenger seat and told it to bark at each traffic light, twice for green and once for red. The dog did pretty well, but unfortunately Bowen couldn't see the white line down the center of the road, so he couldn't keep in lane. He was credited with the 30 days he'd spent in jail awaiting trial, and said he'd given up driving for good.

🔒

IN NORTHERN KENYA, near the Somali border, a 20-year-old man raped a camel in March 1996 and sparked off a brawl, between his relatives and the camel's owner's friends, that left three people injured. A young boy raised the alarm when he spotted the man mounting the camel, having tied its legs and pulled it down to the ground. The rapist fled the scene but was later arrested.

—●

IAN ORD OF BISHOP AUCKLAND, England, was remanded to custody for a retrial in March 1995 on a charge of stealing a car. The retrial was ordered because he couldn't stop laughing in Teesside Crown Court. His lawyer said he suffered from a "nervous disorder."

The case was quite the opposite with Hakic Ceku, a Yugoslavian who appeared in court in Málaga, Spain, in April 1990. Charged with possessing firearms, he didn't make a sound. He'd sewn his lips together to avoid making a statement.

A man tried to fight off six intruders when they burst into his home in Stangby, Sweden, in July 1987. Rather than drive them away, he seems only to have enraged them, and they nailed his foot to the floor while they ransacked his house. The 24-year-old victim was left in agony for hours until a friend found him.

POLICE WERE CALLED to the home of Leland Sallee in Mt. Clemens, Michigan, in May 1991, because his wife claimed Sallee was assaulting her. When they arrived, Sallee beat them with his artificial right arm, mauling one of them with the clawlike pincers at the end of the arm. The prosthesis was later seized as evidence and taken away, thus rendering Sallee "unarmed" until the time of his trial.

From hands to feet: In June 1991, a woman was hijacked in her car by a man waving what looked like a human foot in her face. She was forced to drive 30 miles to Longframlington, England, and then the man ran off.

ONE CAN ONLY IMAGINE the farcical scenes as police tried to quell the riot that occurred at the end of a dinner and disco for deaf mutes in September 1987. It's far from clear what started the trouble, but the 1,500 party-goers hurled beer cans and bottles at the police and sprayed them with foam in a 90-minute rampage following a national convention for the deaf at Blackpool's Winter Gardens. Seventy policemen fought to hold the line before resorting to a direct appeal—using a bullhorn. As the rioters were all deaf and communicating with sign language, this wasn't much help. The trouble was eventually quelled, with four police injuries and seven men charged with disorderly conduct.

—●

LASTLY, FROM THE WEIRD behavior of criminals to that of a Filipino judge: In September 1994, Manila's "hanging judge" Maximiano Asuncion declared that people convicted of crimes carrying the death sentence should be made to wrestle poisonous snakes inside a giant aquarium open to the public.

# The Devil Made Me Do It

Maybe there are hordes of dangerous gods
and demons who tell people what to do.
Maybe some of the people in the following
tales really do come from other planets. On
the other hand...

RICHARD TWINN, 39, appeared in court in February 1982, charged with smashing windowpanes in a door at the home of a former girlfriend in Twickenham, England. However, Twinn, from Kingsthrope, had his excuse ready: He was attempting to save a woman he married in 1991.

Twinn said an inner force made him go to the house, but after waiting around outside for some time, he noticed a telephone booth nearby, and he began to believe he was making an episode of the *Dr. Who* TV series. Conducting his own defense, he said, "I walked inside the telephone booth and thought it was a spaceship or a time machine. When I came out again I checked the date on my watch. The date showed the year 1991." The illusion was further enhanced by a jet flying over with red and green landing lights flashing, and he then decided to smash his way into the house to save the endangered woman inside. He was found guilty of criminal damage and sentenced to 12 months' probation.

BACK IN 1956, Richard Lorenz, 17, was charged with disorderly conduct in connection with several threatening letters sent to a teenage girl. Although the letters were sent from the Niagara Falls, New York, area where Lorenz lived, he claimed the writer was an invisible creature "from a planet in outer space—far out in space—900 trillion miles out in space." One of them ended with an apology for the pencil scrawl: "I don't know why I can't write good when I'm on earth."

SELF-EMPLOYED GARDENER Jeremy Brabrooke, 26, was jailed for life in July 1988 for the murder of Doris Whitaker, 59, at her home in Yorkshire, England. The bearded six-footer was said to have toured Bingley searching for a woman to rape, then forced his way into Whitaker's home and stabbed her nine times with a jackknife when she screamed. The original news report gives a succinct account of his excuse: "Brabrooke claimed he was the reincarnated brother of Conan the Barbarian, that he was turning into an elk, and that he had played for the Leeds United soccer team. A defense psychiatrist said he was crazy."

POLICE IN SHREVEPORT, Louisiana, charged Jake Crawford, 28, with aggravated arson after a house fire in February 1982. Crawford explained that the fire had started when he set light to his teddy bear, which he thought was possessed by demons. Obviously we're dealing with hi-tech demonology here, for he also said that the eyes of the toy were camera lenses, and that the bear was spying on him.

The building was badly damaged in the blaze.

SCHIZOPHRENIC THOMAS MAIN of Camden, England, had not been taking his medication, as a result of which he began to hear the voice of ex-Beatle Paul McCartney telling him "to injure people who whistled." Robert Staunton, 61, was whistling as he walked along the canal towpath in Camden, so Main duly stabbed him in the back. Staunton fell into the canal and was dead before he arrived at the hospital. The hospital was where Main ended up as well.

UNEMPLOYED BRIAN MORROW of Aberdeen, Scotland, admitted a breach of the peace in March 1991 after an incident at a tenement. He had started knocking and kicking at a door to a coal bin, and had been told to go away by the woman who lived in the neighboring apartment, at which point he shouted that he was going to get a sledgehammer. And indeed he did, seeming intent on breaking down the door and freeing the invisible man he believed to be locked in the coal bin. By that time, though, the police had arrived. Morrow was jailed for 60 days and his hammer was taken away.

In Paris, Christophe Van, 39, stabbed his wife, Anna-Maria, 27, with a kitchen knife in August 1990. "She was bewitched by the devil," he told police. "Before I killed her, I looked at my son, the Archangel Gabriel. He approved."

FREELANCE INSURANCE AGENT Adrian Shu Kay Ng, 28, was also a psychopath with six different personalities, each one a Chinese god. When the god of death took him over in January 1984, he ritually beheaded a young mother and then slaughtered her two babies. The murders took place when he visited at the home of Mrs. Mai Tang in Hampton, England, seeking help with his financial difficulties. He was said to be infatuated with Mrs. Tang, who he thought was also immortal and the only woman worthy of his attention. When she refused to help he killed her with a meat cleaver, covered her body in a white sheet, and then killed her children. Then he returned to take photographs of Mrs. Tang's private parts, before tidying the apartment and calling a cab to take him home. Ng pleaded guilty to manslaughter on the grounds of diminished responsibility.

—●

WHEN POLICE WERE CALLED to a newsstand in Croydon, England, in February 1995, they were told that a stranger had gotten into, and was sitting in, a car belonging to a customer. They found Julian Rattray in the driver's seat, and at first he claimed the car was his. Not being believed, he was asked for documents, at which point he started shouting that he was God and came from outer space and didn't need documents. He was persuaded to get out of the car but started shouting again, reaffirming that he was God and could, therefore, do whatever he wished. When he was asked if he had keys for the car, he said God didn't need keys of anything. Appearing in court, "God" proved so omniscient that he couldn't remember his current address, and was sentenced to a year.

---

AUSTIN LEROY WHITE, 35, was detained at a mental-health center in Mississauga, Ontario, in September 1979, after pleading insanity to an arson charge. White, who said he was suffering from a voodoo curse, burned down the house where he was living with his cousin in an attempt to rid himself of a mythical person called "Wally," who was alleged to be haunting him. White said Wally, who apparently lived next door, followed him wherever he went, poisoning his drinks and giving him pains in the head, by putting "oil drops on his brain." In court, White told the judge he would gladly submit to psychiatric help "as long as Wally isn't there."

**In Hitchcock, Texas, 27-year-old Laura McDonald shot and wounded a neighbor's guest in April 1984. When arrested, she explained that the victim, Monette Roseberry, had been "sending electrical charges through the air at her."**

A MILAN COURT HEARD that Egidio Gioia, 28, murdered the wife, son, and mother-in-law of his employer in December 1987 because he was possessed by a demon. Gioia said he murdered Rodolfina Prandini, 37, because she rebuffed his sexual advances, and continued, "I was possessed by her demon, and

St. Nicholas came to me in a dream saying there were only two ways for me to free myself—either to have carnal relations with Rodolfina or to kill her." When asked by the judge why he had also killed her son and mother, Gioia replied, "3, 13 and 17 are magic numbers. Having killed one person, I had to kill the other two." It seems to have run in the family, as psychiatrists testified that Gioia had been raised by two elderly people who believed themselves victims of demonic possession. He was sent to a mental institution.

ROY ZIEGLER OF KITCHENER, Ontario, came to trial March 1986, after he was arrested for driving his moped while drunk and failing to stop for a police patrol car. When Ziegler was eventually brought to a halt, he failed a Breathalyzer test, but he had his excuse ready: He hadn't stopped because he thought he was being pursued by a spaceship. It was an excuse that worked, too, as the judge agreed with him that the car, the rotating red light of which had slipped and was illuminating the interior, could look like a spaceship. The drunken driving and the stolen pair of jeans Ziegler had with him at the time were more difficult to explain, and he was fined $800.

AND LASTLY, A STORY where the Devil really did make him do it. In April 1989, a court in Birmingham, England, was told that Darren Smith, 19, was obsessed with fantasies about the Devil. Getting up one morning at his home in Telford, Shropshire, he found that "there was the writing of Beelzebub on his dressing table," and on the ensuing night he stole a car with a friend. They went joyriding, with Smith driving, and he said that the Devil was on the backseat, laughing and urging him to kill the man cycling ahead of him. The Devil apparently said, "Faster, faster, faster, you have got to kill him." Then, as Smith passed cyclist Martin Childs, the Devil cried, "Now," and Smith deliberately jerked the steering wheel so that he careered into his victim. Childs was left dying in the road, and Smith drove away. Surprisingly enough, in court he was said to be mentally normal.

# M0dern G0thic

Dark crimes, horrid murders, cannibalism
and devil-worship; gather your courage and
hold down your lunch as we recount these
tales of terror.

TWELVE "DEVIL WORSHIPERS" ordered in pizzas from the Buen
Apetito pizza parlor in Buenos Aires, Argentina, in May 1994.
They were delivered to an abandoned factory in a run-down
industrial area of the city by 19-year-old Carlos Sanchez, who
failed to return. His employer reported him missing, and police
raided the factory. Nine of the fiends escaped, but three were
found still dressed in white robes around a candlelit table,
which was strewn with bones. They had ignored the pizzas and
eaten the delivery boy.

A PAIR OF GRIM TALES: A thief stole a box from a car in New
York in April 1992. Opening it, he found six human heads, cut
open for use in research at a medical college. The loot was
dumped in a street 200 yards from the car, and police returned
the heads to the doctor who owned them.

Worse, perhaps, is the following tale from Argentina.
Thieves stole a truck in May 1994, when the driver stopped to
see a friend at a warehouse. Expecting to find $16,000 worth
of meat in the truck, they found 33 human corpses instead. The
cadavers were due to be delivered to a Buenos Aires medical
school, and the truck was found six miles away—its contents
entirely untouched.

IN AUGUST 1995, two teenage girls, Devon Watts and Kelly Heemstra, pulled the trigger of a rifle together and killed an elderly man, then threw a party at his mobile home and showed the corpse to at least ten friends. The girls had been living with 73-year-old Leonard Hughey in White Cloud, Michigan, although precisely why they killed him isn't clear. None of the party-goers contacted police until after the body was found by relatives two days later.

A 40-YEAR-OLD HERDSMAN in the Sokoto State of Nigeria used a drastic remedy when his 12-year-old bride kept running away: He chopped her legs off. She died in the hospital soon after the attack, in December 1986. Despite her husband's protestations that they both loved each other and that he hadn't intended to kill her, he was jailed for life.

IN DECEMBER 1993, American Army Sergeant Stephen Schap walked into a maternity ward in Fulda, Germany, and presented his wife with her lover's decapitated head, telling her: "Look, Diane, Glover is here. He'll sleep with you every night, only you won't sleep at night." Earlier that day, Schap had discovered that the father of his estranged wife's expected baby was Gregory Glover, a fellow mechanic at Sickles Army Air Field. Schap found him in a phone booth and cut off his head with a knife.

WHEN MAURICE JACOBS broke into the morgue at the Albany Medical Center in New York State in December 1990, he apparently didn't like the way the dead had been sewn up. So he left a note implying he could do better and reading "I'm open for a job," signed it, and left his address and telephone number. Security men got in touch and asked him to return to the hospital, but not for a job interview. When he arrived, police arrested him.

A BRIEF TALE from June 1991: Stephen Gagnon, from Alfred, Maine, plucked out a friend's eye in a drug-induced frenzy. He later told police that he had intended to eat the eye, but ended up putting it in his pocket instead.

AT THE END of a 6-month sentence for possession of arms, Swaziland authorities announced that they were deporting the bizarrely named Moroccan Hitler Sharin, a self-confessed cannibal and mercenary, because he had been demanding the bodies of road-accident victims for his meals.

YVONNE KLEINFELDER MURDERED her male roommate by scalding, beating, and starving him to death because he "twisted the little paws" of her four pet cats. John Conner was found lying naked on the floor of her apartment in May 1980, critically burned over 50 percent of his body. He had lain there for six days, unfed, and Kleinfelder had also beaten him with belts and tortured him with lighted cigarettes. "Yvonne boiled me," he told police before he died in the hospital the next day. Kleinfelder apparently once claimed to be "high priestess of a double coven of witches," but later joined a Pentecostal church; exactly what her religion was at the time of the murder is unclear.

Popular hunchback beggar Adamu Kano was hacked to death with machetes behind the mosque in Ijebu-Ode, a town in Nigeria's Ugun State, in September 1995. His murderers cut off his hump, widely believed among the Yoruba to bring good luck.

IN JULY 1995, a Ukrainian man accused of killing a woman and making a bra and shorts out of her skin told a court that he did it to calm his nerves.

CULTISTS DESTROYED 25 tombs in two towns in the province of Agusan del Sur in the southern Philippines on Easter Day in 1994, stealing the kneecaps of the dead in the belief that they could be turned into amulets that protect against bullets. To maximize their effectiveness, it's said, the kneecaps have to be removed at the stroke of midnight on Easter Day. There are numerous similar tales in the *Fortean Times* archives, and this seems to be virtually an annual Easter occurrence somewhere in the Philippines.

In August 1995, kneecap thieves were at it again with quite different motives, with 24 tombs violated in the Philippines town of Bago. It was believed the kneecaps were being ground into powder and burned like incense near a house selected for robbery. The smoke allegedly induces the occupants to fall asleep long enough for the looting to take place.

—◉

THREE TEENAGE BOYS were arrested in September 1995 for killing an old man in Kiev, Ukraine, and cutting off his jaw to steal his gold teeth. When the corpse was discovered, the jaw was found separated from it, wrapped in cloth. The boys had sliced off his jaw with a piece of glass, but later discovered his teeth were not gold but a cheaper metal.

🔒

IN ENGLAND, Susan Goscombe, of no fixed address, pleaded guilty in February 1994 to twice placing huge piles of wood on the Gloucester-to-South Wales railway line. She was hoping to derail the trains so she could "pick the pockets of the dead people." She was committed to Broadmoor mental hospital after psychiatric evidence showed she was mentally ill.

—◉

MALAYSIAN OFFICIALS uncovered a pension fraud scheme in January 1982 involving 567 people of Indian descent. Most had retired from the Malaysian Civil Service and gone home to India, where they continued to receive their checks, which were validated with the recipient's thumbprint. This was all very well until the recipient died, at which point the racketeers stepped in with a simple plan: Cut off the thumb, embalm it, and continue to claim the pension for years thereafter. The Malaysian government was apparently losing $400,000 a year on dead men's thumbs.

🔒

IN THE FLORIDA TOWN of Homestead, 20 miles southwest of Miami, the "biting bandit" made half a dozen attacks at the end of 1989, gnawing fingers, cheeks, and ears off his victims while taking their money. Striking at night, he chewed a finger off one victim to get at a ring, and bit off the ear of another. Detective Jim Pruneda said that after one attack the thief was seen running away with "blood all over his shirt and dripping from his mouth, just like a damned vampire."

A Malaysian man was sentenced to 3 months in Kuala Lumpur in March 1986 after digging up a corpse for guidance in betting on Malaysia's weekly lottery. He took the body into the jungle to pray for winning numbers, but the corpse's selections failed to come up.

AT LEAST TWO MEN broke into the Bohemian National Cemetery in Chicago in February 1990 and tried to open the crypt of a former mayor because they wanted to pose for a photo with his body. Anton Cermak, elected Chicago's mayor in 1928, was assassinated while standing next to U.S. President-elect Franklin Roosevelt in January 1933. Police arrested Mark Moeller on an unrelated burglary charge but found he was carrying a photo of himself and another man standing in front of Cermak's crypt. The remaining offenders were untraced.

🔑

SCRAP DEALER FELIX PERDEREAU was in court in Paris in February 1986, charged with murdering a dead man. He'd gone to a lake on the outskirts of the city to examine the corpse of

Gerard Willekins, another scrap merchant, who had been killed the previous day by Gerard Charaux in an argument over a woman. Perdereau's son had witnessed the crime, but the elder Perdereau suspected that Charaux's blows might only have wounded the victim, so he decided to finish him off. Perdereau bludgeoned the corpse with a metal bar, and even though a postmortem showed that death had occurred 24 hours previously, he was still booked for murder. The court ruled that his intention had clearly been to kill, and he was only prevented from doing so by circumstances beyond his control—that the victim was already dead.

# Sources

## A Bunch Of Bankers

Horne: *Daily Star,* Feb. 18, 1993.
Cooperville: *Daily Record,* Feb. 20, 1993.
Davis: *Bangkok Post,* July 16, 1993.
Vallejo blindman: *Daily Mail,* Mar. 15, 1990.
Florida "bum": *Daily Mail,* Oct. 15, 1980.
Doyle: *Today,* Mar. 13, 1993.
Schmidt: *Wolverhampton Express & Star,* Aug. 23, 1995.
Howells: *Sunday Mail,* Apr. 28, 1991.
Toffeebee: *Sunday People,* Feb. 5, 1995.
Baku: *Guardian,* Apr. 6, 1992.
Mikuni: *Guardian,* Apr. 7, 1993.
Omiya: *Times of Oman,* Dec. 3, 1993.
Nashid: *Int. Herald Tribune,* Apr. 12, 1993.
McFadden: *Jerusalem Post,* June 5, 1994.
Almeida: *Sunday Mail,* May 16, 1993.
Roberts: *Sunday People,* June 19, 1994.
East Hartford: *Waterbury* (Conn.) *Republican,* Aug. 1, 1993.
Hampshire: *Guardian,* July 23, 1992.
Fort Worth. *Int. Herald Tribune,* Dec. 18, 1995.
Macroom: *Aberdeen Press & Journal,* Oct. 9, 1992.
Mainz: *Sunday Mail,* Apr. 23, 1995.
Sunderland: *Daily Telegraph,* Aug. 15, 1992.
Burrell: *Time Out,* Mar. 1995.
Florence: *Wolverhampton Express & Star,* Apr. 21, 1995.
Norton: *New York Daily News,* June 18, 1993.
Gorlach: *Today,* Jan. 12, 1993.
Nicholson: *Daily Mirror,* Aug. 3, 1984.

## Trouble in Store

Philadelphia: *Philadelphia Inquirer,* Apr. 4, 1991.
Los Angeles: *Guardian,* July 10, 1980.
Bunyan: *Daily Star,* Nov. 15, 1980.
Detroit: *Daily Mirror,* Sept. 8, 1984.
Zurich: *Sunday People,* Oct. 19, 1980.
Kemble: *Duluth* (Minn.) *News-Tribune,* Aug. 6, 1995.
Morris: *Daily Telegraph,* Feb. 20, 1986.
Jiwi: *Daily Telegraph,* Jan. 31, 1990.
Alfreton: *Daily Telegraph,* Dec. 5, 1994.
Fubble: *Newcastle Herald,* Mar. 22, 1995.
Rio de Janeiro: *Victoria* (B.C.) *Times-Colonist,* June 14, 1994.
Groningen: *Wolverhampton Express & Star,* July 21, 1995.
Boulder: *Sunday People,* Sept. 12, 1993.
Gregory: *Sun,* Feb. 17, 1983.
Robertson & Fletcher: *Sunday People,* Jan. 1, 1995.
Wilson: *Sun,* Mar. 17, 1992.
Yorkshire: *Sun,* Dec. 11, 1992.
Harris: *Southern Daily Echo,* Mar. 8, 1994.
"Bob": *Victoria* (B.C.) *Times-Colonist,* May 9, 1991.
Sittingbourne: *Daily Mirror,* Mar. 20, 1995.
Lebrom: *Daily Star,* Sept. 25, 1991.
Treadway: *Daily Mirror,* Dec. 19, 1994.

## They Took WHAT?

Arkhangelsk: *Leicester Mercury,* Aug. 31, 1992.
British Rail: *Reveille,* June 9, 1978.

Florida: *Independent,* July 24, 1987.
Duff: *Edinburgh Evening News,* June 1, 1990.
Cobblestones: *Daily Telegraph,* July 15, 1995, etc.
Hartlepool: *Sussex Evening Argus,* Nov. 19, 1994.
Williams: UPI, Mar. 22, 1987.
Hammond: (Nottingham) *Evening Post,* Jan. 2, 1988.
Scarborough: *Daily Telegraph,* Jan. 27, 1988.
Ashton-under-Lyne: *Guardian,* Feb. 22, 1994.
Wantage: *Mail on Sunday,* June 14, 1987.
Leeds: *Guardian,* Oct. 28, 1995.
New Jersey: *Sunday People,* Mar. 6, 1994.
Winnipeg: *Niagara Falls Evening Review,* Nov. 4, 1980.
Phillips: *News of the World,* Oct. 19, 1980.
Holloway: *Daily Telegraph,* Sept. 19, 1981.
Terroni: *Sunday Mail,* June 21, 1992.
Martelli: *Niagara Gazette,* Aug. 15, 1979.
Brynner: *Sunday Mail,* Mar. 1, 1987.
London: *Guardian,* Feb. 8, 1995.
Omonde: (Uganda) *Monitor* , Oct. 9, 1995.
Molatudi: (Harare) *Herald,* Feb. 21, 1996.
Birmingham: *Sussex Evening Argus,* May 15, 1995.
Hatch End: *Ruislip Recorder,* May 18, 1995.

## Felonious Food

Lancaster: *Guardian,* Dec. 11, 1990.
Deck: *Scottish Sunday Mail,* Mar. 28, 1993.
Jabber: *Daily Telegraph,* Nov. 21, 1991.
Sri Lankan woman: *Independent,* Jan. 16, 1996.

Ntima: *Independent on Sunday,* Nov. 6, 1994.
Battering rabbit: *Sunday Mirror,* Aug. 30, 1992.
Buckmeister: *Daily Record,* Aug. 25, 1992.
Hayward: *Daily Mirror,* Jan. 21, 1992.
Gaffney: *Western Daily Press,* Feb. 12, 1992.
Mollica: *Edinburgh Evening News,* Jan. 13, 1994.
Aborigines: *Daily Telegraph,* Mar. 8, 1991, etc.
Saephan: AP, Dec. 17, 1991.
Carrots: *Independent on Sunday,* July 21, 1991.
Cerezo: *Daily Mirror,* June 7, 1989.
Milk truck: *Wolverhampton Express & Star,* Aug. 24, 1995.
Turkish woman: *Sunday Mail,* Sept. 17, 1995.
Lopez: *Sunday Mail,* Jan. 14, 1996.
Cabaso: *St. Louis Post-Dispatch,* Oct. 14, 1984.
Maihof: *Daily Star,* Sept. 29, 1994.
Toothpaste: *Leicester Mercury,* May 25, 1995.
Amestoy: *New York Daily News,* July 14, 1995.
Cream cakes: *Today,* June 21, 1995.
"Hungry Ninja Bandit": *New York Daily News,* May 5, 1988.
Johnson: *Lincoln Standard,* Aug. 28, 1992.

## All Dressed Up, and...

Muppets: *News of the World,* Dec. 31, 1978.
Mongo: *St. Louis Post-Dispatch,* June 30, 1983; *St. Louis Globe-Democrat,* Oct. 7, 1983.
Devil: (Australia) *Sun:* Oct. 17, 1978.
Briggs: (Tucson, Ariz.) *Daily Star,* Aug. 25, 1991.
Easter Bunny: (London) *Times,* Apr. 21, 1987.

Mr. Twister: *Evening Standard,* Oct. 27, 1995.

Ghosts: *Independent,* Aug. 7, 1992.

Hudson: *Sunday Express,* Apr. 13, 1986.

Duff: *Daily Telegraph,* Jan. 3, 1987.

Cat man: *Middlesbrough Evening Gazette,* Nov. 2, 1990.

Collins: *Australian,* Nov. 1978.

Midget: *Daily Record,* Apr. 22, 1994.

Superheroes: (Portsmouth) *News,* Nov. 9, 1985.

Batman: *Daily Mirror,* Feb. 10, 1990.

Horse head: *Welland* (Ont.) *Tribune,* July 30, 1914.

Walker: *Stars & Stripes,* July 26, 1993.

Lunden: *Daily Mirror,* Dec. 20, 1980.

Phillippi: *Beaumont* (Tex.) *Enterprise,* Jan. 5, 1984.

Box & bag: *London Australian Magazine,* Aug. 26–Sept. 1, 1980.

## Four-Wheel Fumbles

Amherst: (Canada) *Globe & Mail,* Feb. 5, 1980.

Wideawake: *Sun,* Nov. 3, 1994.

Harrison: *Hartford* (Conn.) *Courant,* Dec. 30, 1994.

Lambert: *Daily Mail,* Mar. 28, 1995.

Fort Lauderdale: *Sunday Express,* Feb. 26, 1995.

de Melo: *Edinburgh Evening Argus,* July 16, 1991.

Cyprian: *Int. Herald Tribune,* June 5, 1995.

Sutton Coldfield: *Sussex Evening Argus,* May 29, 1995.

Jagla: *Sussex Evening Argus,* May 15, 1993.

Amsterdam: *Guardian,* Mar. 23, 1994.

Milan: *Daily Record,* Jan. 28, 1994.

Mansfield: *Sussex Evening Argus,* May 28, 1993.

Rhode Island: *Daily Record,* May 20, 1993.

South Africa; *Daily Telegraph,* Sept. 5, 1995.

Arlington: *Guardian,* May 30, 1995.

Davies: *Sussex Evening Argus,* Oct. 6, 1994.

Somerset: *Daily Mirror,* Mar. 28, 1991.

Hanna: *Daily Mirror,* Apr. 12, 1991.

Demma: *South China Morning Post,* May 7, 1992.

Root: *Int. Herald Tribune,* Sept. 13, 1993.

Riley: *Daily Star,* June 8, 1994.

South Yorkshire: *News of the World,* Oct. 25, 1992.

Desautelle: *New York Daily News,* Aug. 16, 1992.

Howard: *South Devon Herald Express,* June 11, 1994.

Florence: *Sunday Express,* Aug. 18, 1985.

Bologna: *Car and Driver,* Feb. 1992.

Edinburgh: *Guardian,* Jan.5, 1991.

Gloucestershire: *Daily Star,* Jan. 14, 1994.

Araujo: *Bangkok Post,* Aug. 8, 1994.

## In Strictest Confidence

Serge: *European,* Oct. 8–11, 1992.

Skylab: *Weekly News,* Aug. 4, 1979.

Moon Water: *Weekly News,* Dec. 23, 1995.

Madame Lim: (Malaysia) *Star,* May 23, 1988.

Brock: AP, Apr. 8, 1995.

Jing: *Guardian,* Feb. 13, 1989.

Dissolving checks: *USA Today,* Mar. 25, 1988.

MR: (Johannesburg) *Star,* Feb. 15, 1991.

Aavold: *Daily Record,* Oct. 10, 1995.

Mafia: *Sunday People,* Oct. 9, 1983.

Olatoyosi: *Europa Times,* May 1994.

Wakelin: (Bristol) *Evening Post,* May 13, 1995.

Iranian: *Sunday Telegraph,* Aug. 27, 1995.

Xerxes: *Edinburgh Evening News,* May 4, 1994.

Orangutans: *Sunday People,* Sept. 11, 1994.

Khranthaworn: *Sun,* Oct. 14, 1994.

McCormick: *Sun,* Dec. 12, 1988.

Statue of Liberty: *Scottish Sunday Mail,* Feb. 10, 1991.

# Bungling Burglars

Dos Santos: *Times of Malta,* Jan. 15, 1994.

Woolley: *Sacramento Bee,* Dec. 15, 1995.

Durban: (Sydney) *Sun,* Oct. 30, 1978.

São Paulo: *Guardian,* Mar. 10, 1984.

Oates: *Milton Keynes Herald & Post,* Aug. 22, 1991.

Morales: AP, Jan. 5, 1993.

Koloini: *Sunday Express,* Aug. 11, 1995.

Brown: *Sun,* Mar. 27, 1984.

Walcott: *Sun,* Nov. 28, 1984.

Bridgend: *Daily Telegraph,* July 8, 1988.

Ceglie: *Sunday Express,* July 13, 1986.

South Marston: *Guardian,* Jan. 30, 1996.

Jones: *Norfolk* (Va.) *Virginian-Pilot,* May 21, 1993.

Amsterdam: *Times of Oman,* Mar. 7, 1994.

Bishopsgate: *Wolverhampton Express & Star,* Oct. 13, 1994.

Southport: *Independent,* June 20, 1995.

Kuala Lumpur: *Sunday Express,* Aug. 20, 1995.

Smart: *Newcastle Evening Chronicle,* Apr. 13, 1994.

Spangler: *San Jose Mercury News,* Oct. 10, 1993.

Darby & Jones: *Daily Express,* Jan. 5, 1994.

Bristol: *Daily Telegraph,* Sept. 8, 1992.

Guimaires: *Guardian,* Mar. 29, 1996.

Munich. *Daily Record,* Sept. 3, 1993.

Laidler: *Sunday People,* Jan. 16, 1994.

Hartman: *Philadelphia Inquirer,* Aug. 1, 1994.

Darlington: *Daily Mail,* Jan. 10, 1996.

New York: *Daily Record,* Sept. 12, 1992.

Rio de Janeiro: *Times of Malta,* Mar. 2, 1994.

Carrasco: *Philadelphia Inquirer,* Mar. 19, 1992.

# Safety First?

Chichester: *Daily Mirror,* Aug. 26, 1980.

Munkebo: *Daily Mirror,* June 9, 1987.

Littlehampton: *Sussex Evening Argus,* May 21, 1993.

Sydney: *Sunday Mail,* Apr. 14, 1991.

Wiltshire: *Times of Malta,* Apr. 28, 1994.

Dorset: *Daily Star,* Mar. 20, 1992.

Bielefeld: *Reveille,* Feb. 9, 1979.

Dordrecht: *Sunday Mail,* Apr. 14, 1991.

Kyrenia: *Daily Record,* May 27, 1994.

Weitendorf: *Guardian,* July 16, 1984.

Southend: *Times,* Dec. 26, 1994.

Douglas: *Daily Post,* Mar. 8, 1994.

Brede: *Daily Record,* Dec. 15, 1994.

Wakefield: *Daily Mirror,* June 9, 1984.

Nowra: (Brisbane) *Courier Mail,* Dec. 1, 1993.

Bedminster: *Guardian,* Mar. 31, 1994.

## Mugs And Muggers

Morse: *Daily Record,* Mar. 13, 1993.

Levubu: *Daily Telegraph,* Oct. 11, 1984.

Kettle: *Sunday Telegraph,* Jan. 7, 1996.

Solihull: *Morning Star,* Feb. 28, 1995.

Leeds: *Yorkshire on Sunday,* Nov. 14, 1993.

Bracknell: *Sun,* Oct. 27, 1992.

Essex: *Daily Telegraph,* Sept. 2, 1992.

Brewer: *South Wales Echo,* June 8, 1990.

Gland & Williams: *New York Post,* Aug. 12, 1994.

W. Virginia: *Sun,* Mar. 26, 1994.

Smith: *Akron* (Ohio) *Beacon-Journal,* Mar. 1, 1991.

Pouchin: *Daily Star,* Aug. 21, 1993.

Osaka: *Sunday Express,* Oct. 30, 1994.

Coates: *Int. Herald Tribune,* Mar. 6, 1996.

Johannesburg: *Sun,* Apr. 23, 1992.

Bari: *Aberdeen Press & Journal,* Aug. 11, 1995.

Brussels: *Independent,* Apr. 6, 1996.

Telford: *Daily Mirror,* Sept. 2, 1994.

Charles: *Sunday People,* May 8, 1994.

Gunning: *Daily Telegraph,* July 18, Nov. 3, 1995.

Tomasello: *Europa Times,* June 1994.

Stiller: (Hackensack, N.J.) *Record,* Apr. 4, 1995.

Southsea: *Daily Mirror,* June 1, 1993.

Cunningham: *New York Times,* Aug. 24, 1992.

Sydenham: *South London Press,* Feb. 21, 1992.

## Not-So-Clean Getaways

Acree: *USA Today,* Apr. 8, 1993.

Sapporo: *Sunday Devon Herald Express,* Aug. 26, 1994.

Dodsworth: *Daily Mirror,* Oct. 27, 1993.

Ellis: (Portsmouth) *News,* Mar. 29, 1990.

Berne: *Daily Star,* Sept. 24, 1992.

Green: *Daily Star,* Nov. 27, 1992.

Ballard: (Brisbane) *Courier Mail,* Jan. 31, 1992.

Gillis: *New York Daily News,* Apr. 19, 1992.

Birmingham: *Leicester Mercury,* Mar. 4, 1995.

Washington: *Edinburgh Evening News,* Dec. 10, 1993.

Hawke: *Sunday Mail,* June 13, 1993.

Los Angeles: *Sunday Mail,* Aug. 24, 1995.

Ellis: *Sun,* Sept. 1, 1993.

Williams: *St. Louis Post-Dispatch,* Mar. 6, 1994.

## Just Their Luck

Saanich: *Victoria* (B.C.) *Times-Colonist,* Aug. 21, 1992.

Shidler: *Lancaster* (Pa.) *New Era,* July 23, 1994.

Snyder: *Birmingham* (England) *Evening Mail,* Dec. 21, 1971.

Ortez: *Victoria* (B.C.) *Times-Colonist,* July 9, 1993.

Burkitt: *Today,* Feb. 1, 1992.

Hunter: *Arizona Daily Star,* Feb. 2, 1991.

Beresford: *Western Morning News,* Oct. 30, 1993.

Pederson: *Sunday Express,* Sept. 23, 1990.

Skinner: *Daily Star,* Feb. 18, 1994.

Abdullah: *Sunday Mail,* Jan. 10, 1993.

James: *Augusta* (Ga.) *Chronicle,* Feb. 6, 1985.

Stockton-on-Tees: *Edinburgh Evening News,* Feb. 2, 1994.

# It's the Law!

Hartford: *Int. Herald Tribune,* Jan. 9, 1991.

Nash: (Clwyd & Chester) *Evening Leader,* June 10, 1992.

Southend: *Evening News,* Oct. 20, 1980.

Braggs: *Daily Mail,* Feb. 14, 1987.

Pace: (Johannesburg) *People,* Jan. 16, 1991.

Zappalla: *Sunday People,* Nov. 7, 1993.

Bangkok: *Sussex Evening Argus,* Nov. 3, 1994.

Napolitano: *New York Post,* Feb. 17, 1994.

Nice: *Daily Record,* Sept. 3, 1993.

Berry: *East London Advertiser,* Oct. 5, 1995.

Bloomfield: *Daily Telegraph,* Nov. 16, 1988.

Palumbo: *Sunday Express,* Sept. 17, 1995.

Bilsborough: *Daily Telegraph,* Sept. 9, 1995.

Dorsey: *New York News,* July 8, 1993.

Edmonds: *Guardian,* July 17, 1992.

Middlesbrough: *Daily Express,* Nov. 20, 1993.

Velez: *Sunday Express,* Dec. 11, 1994.

Langan: *Augusta* (Ga.) *Chronicle,* Feb. 18, 1996.

Gilmer: *Yorkshire Evening Post,* Feb. 23, 1995.

Campbell: *Bangkok Post,* Aug. 29, 1994.

Wynn: (Lewiston, Me.) *Sun-Journal,* Dec. 21, 1995.

Kenyon: *Daily Mirror,* May 28, 1986.

Mafua: *Independent,* Jan. 11, 1996.

Indianapolis: *Scotsman,* Mar. 12, 1986.

Kinsella: *Kitchener* (Ont.) *Record,* Nov. 23, 1994.

Melo: *Independent,* July 12, 1995.

Almeida & da Silva: *Philadelphia Inquirer,* Dec. 18, 1993.

Michell: *Lancaster* (Pa.) *New Era,* Aug. 3, 1991.

Jorgen: *Guardian,* Jan. 9, 1991.

Pecs: *Guardian,* Feb. 19, 1993.

Mitchem: *Sunday Express,* Oct. 29, 1995, etc.

Taylor: (Lewiston, Me.) *Sun-Journal,* Jan. 29, 1994.

Washington: *Sun,* Feb. 26, 1992.

Stafford: *Daily Telegraph,* Dec. 30, 1993.

Jardon & Viar: *Daily Express,* Sept. 8, 1993.

Hall: *Guardian,* July 23, 1995.

Graham: *Sunday Express,* Oct. 30, 1994.

Brown: *Daily Record,* Mar. 29, 1993.

Calaya: *Sunday Mail,* Feb. 26, 1995.

Aix-en-Provence: *European,* July 22, 1993.

Chelmsford: *Daily Mirror,* Dec. 13, 1994.

Johnston: *Daily Telegraph,* Sept. 29, 1994.

Barrett: *Sierra Vista* (Ariz.) *Herald,* Dec. 29, 1991, etc.

Bissel, Sledge, & Castleberry: *Hartford* (Conn.) *Courant,* Nov. 8, 1994.

# Escape Artists

Shepard: *Independent on Sunday,* July 3, 1994.

Watford: *Guardian,* Sept. 4, 1985.

Abdullah: *Daily Mirror,* Jan. 28, 1985.

Logan: *Sun,* Oct. 10, 1985.

# Not the Straight Dope

Kleschinski: *New York Daily News,* Dec. 28, 1995.

Ventham: *Daily Telegraph,* Aug. 27, 1994.

Dutch dealer: *Guardian,* Nov. 15, 1995.

Collins: *Atlanta Constitution*, Mar. 27, 1990.

Plumley: *USA Today*, Dec. 12, 1995.

Salisbury: *San Jose Mercury News*, June 22, 1993.

McGuire: (Brisbane) *Courier Mail*, June 27, 1992.

Trujillo: *Daily Record*, Sept. 22, 1995.

Denver: *Denver Post*, Dec. 26, 1993.

Tiang Ponpa: *Bangkok Post*, Oct. 28, 1992.

Rio de Janeiro: *Sun*, Aug. 26, 1995.

Customs: *Daily Telegraph*, Sept. 26, 1994.

Amsterdam: *Wolverhampton Express & Star*, Dec. 28, 1995.

Rabat: Reuters, Mar. 2, 1994.

Essex: *Today*, Sept. 24, 1993.

San Diego: *Weekly News*, Aug. 19, 1978.

Walder: *Leicester Mercury*, Apr. 21, 1995.

Thailand: Reuters, Dec. 29, 1992.

Michigan: *Daily Record*, Feb. 9, 1994.

Laberge: *Rocky Mountain News*, Apr. 29, 1992.

Mortenson: AP, Nov. 8, 1991.

## Bizarre Break-Ins

Living-room door: *Weekly News*, Sept. 28, 1974.

Pescay: *Sussex Express*, July 7, 1995.

Bedsheets: *Sunday People*, Jan. 31, 1988.

Knife & fork: *Daily Telegraph*, Oct. 7, 1982.

Masai tribesman: *Daily Telegraph*, Feb. 14, 1984.

Holland: *Daily Mirror*, June 2, 1992.

Mills: *Daily Mirror*, Sept. 11, 1987.

Prince Eddie: *Los Angeles Times*, Oct. 22, 1987.

Boykins: *Augusta* (Ga.) *Herald*, July 18, 1990.

Collingwood: *Edinburgh Evening News*, Aug. 7, 1992.

Radlich: AP, June 4, 1993.

Yu Kin-fong: *Guardian*, Dec. 17, 1994.

Toler: *Daily Mail*, Sept. 2, 1982.

False teeth: *Daily Telegraph*, Oct. 19, 1983.

Lewis: *Times of Oman*, May 9, 1994.

Baby fetishist: *Sunday People*, Mar. 27, 1994.

Smillie: *Daily Telegraph*, June 16, 1995.

Brown: *Daily Record*, Feb. 5, 1996.

Loganville burglar: *Atlanta Journal*, July 31, 1993.

Rochdale school: *Sussex Evening Argus*, Mar. 16, 1995.

Burglar alarm: *Daily Telegraph*, Feb. 13, 1982.

Kettering police: *Daily Telegraph*, Jan. 21, 1995.

Brooklyn jail: *New York Daily News*, May 3, 1986.

Wyman & Walters: *Guardian*, Nov. 6, 1991.

## The Mad and the Bad

Lorentzos: *Daily Telegraph*, Jan. 31, 1981.

Honolulu: *Houston Chronicle*, Dec. 19, 1982.

Baldesi: *Sunday Express*, Dec. 30, 1984.

Tokyo: *Guardian*, Apr. 28, 1987.

Rosenbaum: *Midweek*, Jan. 23, 1992.

Chicago: *Daily Mail*, Dec. 29, 1984.

Justice: AP, June 22, 1995.

Maestrini: *Sunday People*, Mar. 6, 1994.

Melbourne: *Guardian*, June 27, 1992.

McFarlane: *New Zealand News*, Nov. 22, 1995.

Wanganui: *Evening Standard*, Mar. 22, 1996.

Mulder: *Daily Record*, June 7, 1995.
Bury St. Edmunds: *Daily Record*, Oct. 10, 1994.
Loyd: AP, Jan. 27, 1982.
Davey: *Halifax Evening Courier*, Oct. 11, 1995.
Brownless: *Independent*, June 7, 1995.
Bowen: *Cleveland Plain Dealer*, July 2, 1986.
Kenya: *Jakarta Post*, Mar. 20, 1996.
Ord: *Daily Telegraph*, Mar. 17, 1995.
Ceku: *Daily Telegraph*, Apr. 20, 1990.
Stangby: *Today*, July 6, 1987.
Sallee: *Newsweek*, May 13, 1991.
Longframlington: *Daily Mirror*, June 14, 1991.
Blackpool: *Daily Mirror*, Sept. 15, 1987.
Asuncion: *Daily Telegraph*, Sept. 12 1994.

## The Devil Made Me Do It

Twinn: *Daily Telegraph*, Feb. 10, 1982.
Lorenz: *Niagara Falls Evening Review*, Feb. 13, 1956.
Brabrooke: *Daily Telegraph*, July 28, 1988.
Crawford: *Daily Telegraph*, Feb. 12, 1982.
Main: *Daily Mirror*, Dec. 14, 1990.
Morrow: *Daily Record*, Mar. 27, 1991.
Van: *Bild* (Germany), Aug. 14, 1990.
Ng: *Daily Mirror*, Nov. 14, 1987.
Rattray: *Croydon Post, Feb.* 8, 1995.
White: *Mississauga* (Ont.) *News*, Sept. 19, 1979.
McDonald: *Portland* (Me.), *Press Herald*, Apr. 4, 1984.
Gioia: *Wolverhampton Express & Star*, Dec. 3, 1987.
Ziegler: *Niagara Falls Evening Review*, Mar. 19, 1986.
Smith: *Daily Mail*, Apr. 11, 1989.

## Modern Gothic

Sanchez: *Wolverhampton Express & Star*, June 1, 1994.
New York: *Sun*, Apr. 16, 1992.
Buenos Aires: *Daily Star*, May 19, 1995.
Watts & Heemstra: *Wolverhampton Express & Star*, Aug. 2, 1995.
Sokoto: *Daily Mirror*, Sept. 28, 1987.
Schap: AP, Dec. 9, 1993.
Jacobs: *New York Post*, Dec. 1990.
Gagnon: *Independent*, June 28, 1991.
Sharin: *Guardian*, Dec. 22, 1990.
Kleinfelder: *Toronto Sun*, Dec. 11, 1980.
Kano: AP, Sept. 21, 1995.
Ukrainian murderer: AP, July 6, 1995.
Philippines: *Gulf News*, Apr. 12, 1994; *Yorkshire Post*, Aug. 7, 1995; etc.
Kiev: *Scotsman*, Sept. 20, 1995.
Goscombe: *Daily Record*, Feb. 11, 1994.
Malaysian thumbs: *Daily Telegraph*, Jan. 4, 1982.
Pruneda: *Independent*, Jan. 9, 1990.
Kuala Lumpur: *Guardian*, Mar. 14, 1986.
Moeller: *Toronto Sun*, Feb. 10, 1990.
Perdereau: *Daily Express*, Feb. 19, 1986.

# READY FOR A DOSE OF WEIRDNESS?

ISBN: 0-8362-1499-4      ISBN: 0-8362-2767-0      ISBN: 0-8362-2147-8

No one knows more about separating the certifiably quirky from the merely quotidian than the *Fortean Times*. *Strange Days #1* and *Strange Days #2* show exactly how weird the world is and have the evidence to back it up. Divided into chapters such as "Alien Abductions," "Hoaxes and Panics," "Crop Circles," and "Spontaneous Human Combustion," the *Strange Days* volumes employ the *FT* Strangeness Index to quantify the annual weirdness factor. They also present ground-breaking research, nailing down the science behind everything from reports of falling goo in Oakville, Washington, to widespread reports of a dwarf cyclops batman terrorizing the citizens of Zanzibar. More than just a catalog of the bizarre and bewildering, these are diaries of a mad planet.

*The Comedian Who Choked to Death on a Pie . . . and the Man who Quit Smoking at 116* is a compendium of true tales of the hilarious deaths and bizarrely triumphant lives of ordinary folks from around the world. This book gathers together hundreds of comic demises with a cast of over 50 centenarians, revealing fascinating and funny insights into how to live, and how not to.

The mysteries, curiosities, prodigies and portents gathered in every *Fortean Times* book come from real news clips gathered by hundreds of stringers in 35 countries around the globe.

From UFOs, Bigfoot and visions of the Virgin Mary to weird tales and human oddities, *Fortean Times* is a respected chronicler of strange phenomena with 24 years' experience of reporting from wild frontiers. Informed, open-minded, skeptical and above all extremely funny, *FT* has the low-down on what's out there.

Write or call for details of our latest subscription offers. Or send for a sample issue for just $4.95. (You can pay by credit card using our order hotline, or with a check payable to Fenner, Reed & Jackson.)

Fortean Times
Box 754
Manhasset, NY 11030-0754
Phone: (516) 627-3836 Fax: (516) 627-1972.
E-mail: sgrudnick@aol.com